POST WAR

THE FILMS OF DANIEL EISENBERG

Edited by Jeffrey Skoller

black dog publishing

london uk

CONTENTS

POSTWAR
INTRODUCTION

Jeffrey Skoller

**Always returning upon the paths of time, we are neither ahead nor behind:
late is early, near far.**
Maurice Blanchot

The cinema of Daniel Eisenberg makes the present waiver. His films reverberate across time, bringing the events of the past into a present constituted by constant flux. In his work, Eisenberg is preoccupied with the ways past events continue to accrue new meanings and power as they move through time, across cities, continents, political and personal geographies. These rigorously formal films are timepieces that are at once documents of the dynamic present, and an interrogation of the meanings produced from the materials our culture uses to connect to the flow of time.

POSTWAR: The films of Daniel Eisenberg is the first major critical study of this unique American filmmaker who began making films in the late 1970s. Rather than a mid-career survey, this volume focuses on Eisenberg's four thematically connected films, made between 1981 and 2003, which when taken together, trace the on-going implications of the events of the Second World War and the fall of the Berlin Wall—the structuring political events of the second half of the twentieth century—and continue into the twenty-first. Refusing to join in the popular claims of the "end of history" that has characterized the rhetorics of closure and a break with the past of the Cold War period in the midst of geo-political restructuring and economic globalization, Eisenberg instead explores the ways these events continue to unfold as structuring elements of the personal and political present. As works of visual history, the films engage contemporary questions about the nature of time—relationships between past, present and the future—the transformation of the meanings of events over time and the problems of representing those elements of past events that defy coherent narrativization.

Unabashedly ambitious and serious, the themes of Eisenberg's films emerge from his personal experience. Born the child of survivors of the Shoah in the aftermath of the Second World War, his growing awareness of the world—like many Eastern European Jews just after the war—existed in a liminal space between Europe, Israel and the United States. The films can be seen as a cognitive mapping of the ways that the effects of the catastrophe of Europe continues into the contemporary political and cultural moment in the most deeply personal and aesthetic ways. Stylistically,

Eisenberg's films also occupy an equally liminal space between several recognizable genres, often making them hard to categorize. Never fitting neatly into any single approach, the films can be seen as hybrid and stylistically tactical, appropriating different forms as necessary to explore specific questions. As such, they are in dialogue with the personal, formalist cinema of the American Avant-Garde such as Yvonne Rainer, Ernie Gehr and James Benning, as well as the historical documentary of Patricio Guzman, Marcel Ophüls and Péter Forgács and the film essay forms of the European art cinema such as Chris Marker, Harun Farocki, and Chantal Akerman. In his films, Eisenberg explores the contemporary landscape in which visible objects such as museums, archives, statues, churches, synagogues, prisons, concentration camps, monuments and cities are revealed as temporal strata. Such strata embody different moments in time which are juxtaposed and intersect in ways that often open onto the unseen, causing us to consider the dynamic energies of history that permeate its visible artifacts. We see public spaces of the city in permanent flux, as buildings are razed, restored or in decay, while other sites are transformed in more ephemeral ways by the changing light of day and night or by the passage of a train moving across the carefully composed frame of a cityscape. Eisenberg integrates documents and objects from the past into his landscapes of the present—forgotten film footage found in military archives, or detourned from other films, old family photographs and identity cards. We hear on the film's sound tracks personal stories, aphorisms, music, eyewitness accounts, and silence. The complex interplay between the concrete experience of seeing what is actually on the screen and other ephemeral experiences such as thought, affect, memory, desire or bodily sensation that often defy representation, emerge beyond the frame through juxtaposition of diverse elements and produce a unique spectral temporality between past, present, and even the future. Such virtualities are sensed, but remain unapprehendable. Nevertheless they are part of the energy of the past and exert themselves as a force on the present. The attempt to bring such unseen forces into relationship with what can be seen and heard defines the challenge of his unique work.

Eisenberg began making films as a college student in the 1970s during the most radically open and experimental period in the history of cinema, a time when it was taken as axiomatic that formal experimentation had to be an integral part of a progressive aesthetic practice. Central to the independent film culture of the time was the radical aspiration that we could use film to ask the deepest and most relevant questions that we face in our lives, that new forms had to be invented to explore the most crucial questions of the time, and that the medium was actually capable of answering those questions.

In the United States, access to the technologies to make films was largely located in the universities. Eisenberg studied at the State University of New York at Binghamton just as the study and practice of media as a fine art was entering the academy. The pioneering Avant-Garde filmmaker Ken Jacobs, along with his colleague Larry Gottheim, created a filmmaking program there based upon the artisanal practices of the New American Cinema. The emphasis at the time was on the material exploration of the film medium and its possibilities as a medium for personal visual expression. Experimentation with the ways film mediates reality rather than represents it was at the center of much of the creative work that challenged dominant conventions of dramatic and documentary film forms.

In this context the filmmaker was the sole producer, often filming, recording sound and editing each film himself. This shift away from collaborative production not only emphasized the filmmaker's personal relationship to the crafting of the film, but extended into its themes. The integration of an expressive and highly personal relationship to every aspect of production created a new sense of what filmmaking could be, both as autobiography and as an evolved aesthetic of subjective and perceptual exploration. In addition to Jacobs, filmmakers from Stan Brakhage, Jonas Mekas and Maya Deren to Hollis Frampton, Ernie Gehr and Yvonne Rainer were central figures in this vein.

For filmmakers of Eisenberg's generation, the growing awareness of European avant-garde film practices in the 1970s also played a decisive role the development of the post-70s American Avant-Garde. Filmmakers from Straub/Huillet, Alexander Kluge, Ulrike Ottinger, to Chantal Akerman, Jean-Luc Godard and Chris Marker, were exploring the formal problems of how to adequately narrate the past of post-war Europe in all of its cultural and geo-political complexities. These European practices differed from the American Avant-Garde both in their modes of production and in the interrogation of more overt representations of social and political subject matter. Like Eisenberg, many of his generation of filmmakers who studied film in the academy had become more theoretically informed with the emergence of cultural studies and were influenced by a wide range of non-cinematic and fine art disciplines such as sociology, anthropology, film and critical theory, historiography, post-colonial, feminist and queer studies and began to address them in their films. Filmmakers such as Leslie Thornton, Su Friedrich, Rea Tajiri, Isaac Julian, Craig Baldwin, Trinh T. Minh-Ha, Gregg Bordowitz, Jennifer Montgomery and others can be seen as part of an emerging hybrid avant-garde cinema of mixed styles and forms. As I have suggested elsewhere Eisenberg, and his generation can be seen as part of a third avant-garde to emerge in the 1980s.

Along side of these experimental practices, during this period Eisenberg began working professionally as a film editor and researcher for National Public Television on several important social history documentary film projects including *Eyes on the Prize*, a 14-hour documentary series on the African American Civil Rights Movement, and *Vietnam: A Television History*, a 13-part visual history of the war. These works worked heavily with archival film images and, as Eisenberg himself writes in the final essay in this book, that experience played an important part in how he approaches the use of such historical documents.

Fluent in all of these forms and approaches, Eisenberg uses as necessary, elements of the personal diary film, the historical documentary, the found footage film, the film essay and observational documentary. The result is a body of work which is not easily classifiable. At once formally rigorous and stylistically promiscuous, Eisenberg uses these forms as a vocabulary to produce different modes of attention, to highlight the ways constellations of events, experiences, and objects produce complex discursive meanings rather than univocal narratives molded into of causalities or inevitabilities. Eisenberg's films are never closed cinematic objects designed to be admired for their beauty (although they are beautiful) or for their craftsmanship (although they are masterfully filmed and edited), they are designed to be interacted with, responded to, conversed with.

In his work, Eisenberg uses his own existence as a pivot point where past and present intersect. Inspired by a visit to Paris, in *Displaced Person*, 1981, he uses a scrap of archival footage of Hitler surveying La Madeleine in Paris to interrogate the image of the edifice as a temporal intersection between himself-as a tourist in the 1980s—and the figure who destroyed much of his family 40 years earlier, standing exactly in the same place. Similarly in *Cooperation of Parts*, 1987, he returns to the apartment complex in Poland where his mother lived before the war and to the concentration camps to which she was deported. Again he scrutinizes these sites to contemplate the intersection between her past in one historical context and his present in another. In *Persistence*, 1997, and *Something More Than Night,* 2003, Eisenberg explores the transformations of the urban metropolis in Berlin and Chicago respectively. As time-strata, the cities themselves embody the diachronic nature of historical change. In their constant demolition and renovation, they reveal how society is constantly adjusting and adapting to the ways past events continue to be part of the present. Thus 'postwar' is redefined to mean something more complex than the end of war. Taken as a whole, the quartet of films becomes an image of what that term might mean.

FROM FILM TO BOOK: A TRANSPOSITION

In thinking about how to create a book on these highly cinematic works, our intention was to not to make a simple document of the films via a series of academic essays, but to make something of that could exist alongside the films as an elaboration of them. While the specificity of the film medium—how it produces distinct experience, is central to the aesthetics of Eisenberg's films, we asked in what ways might their transposition to another medium—a paper book of images and text—produce new thoughts through a different kind of dialogue with the films. One thinks of other examples of this impulse in Chantal Akerman's experiments transposing her single screen films such as *D'est*, 1993, and others into multi-screen installations that moved the works out of the film theatre and into the more open and mobile space of the museum.

At the same time we wanted bring this unique quartet of films to greater public attention and show how the tradition of experimental cinema is not just one of continuing technological or stylistic innovation, but also of deeply intellectual exploration through images and sound. In order to do this, we invited a range of distinguished film scholars, cultural theorists and historians to write along side of and in dialogue with the films, deepening our understanding of these complex works while expanding upon the ideas they place in motion. Working with these wonderful essays, Eisenberg and I embarked on an extraordinarily rewarding collaboration using still images from the films along with images and documents from other sources to surround the writings. Again our intention was not merely to illustrate the texts with images, but to create new kinds of juxtapositions in which there is a dynamic relationship between what is written and what is seen. At times, the texts serve as catalysts to activate the image collages that run through the book, and at other points the images give the texts a visual dimension, elaborating and deepening the writer's ideas, and in still other places the images appear on their own, to be read and seen as objects in their own right.

The essays themselves can be seen as a guide to these often difficult works, to be read in conjunction with their viewing. In his introductory essay "Persistent Displacements: The City Films of Dan Eisenberg", film historian Tom Gunning gives a detailed overview of the four works and their intersecting themes, showing how deeply imbued they are with the history of modernist art. He connects the films to the traditions of the avant-garde "city symphony" and other modernist evocations of the city in painting, poetry and architecture which show it as the site of historical revelation and futurist aspiration, at times utopian and at others catastrophic. Like the films themselves, Gunning moves back and forth in time, showing how the history of modern art itself becomes part of the temporal strata of the present Eisenberg is exploring. Gunning also explores the different forms and themes that each film employs while convincingly showing how in aggregate the films are "a series of interwoven threads", each film illuminating different aspects of the same series of questions. Each of the other six essays focuses on a single film in the quartet. As a collection however, they are fugue-like in the ways they focus on different facets of individual films, yet often causing the same images and ideas to return from essay to essay to be seen and understood in different ways. Repetition and transformation, a critical strategy within and between the films themselves, is recapitulated here between essays as well.

There are two essays on the first film in the four, *Displaced Person*, 1981. French film theorist Raymond Bellour's essay "Kids on a Bike" is a highly personal meditation, focusing on a single image of two boys on a bicycle that is repeated throughout the film. Bellour works to articulate the ways Eisenberg's treatment of this image evokes a particular affective response, tapping into his own childhood memories. Bellour poetically explores the on-going enigma of how the energies of certain moving images—even without detailed knowledge of what they are or where they came from—can open onto very deep parts of our psyches, while others remain inert. Focusing on the equally important use of music and spoken language in *Displaced Person*, film historian Nora Alter's "Sound Scores: Musical Armature in *Displaced Person*", shows how Eisenberg's use of music—Beethoven's *String Quartet #9, Opus 59 in C major #3*, 1808—opens onto another temporal space that surrounds and structures The viewer's relation to the images. This virtual space not only evokes the history and cultural context of which the music is a signifier, but it also generates an affective experience that transforms the images. As she writes… "[with] the soundtrack another story emerges, a narrative which is sometimes contradictory, and at times parallel, or sometimes in synch with the images, but always it contains its own line of meaning". Similarly in a lecture fragment in English by the French anthropologist Claude Lévi-Strauss heard over the film's images, the "grain" of his voice, its timbre, accent, rhythms, and intonation as the voice of rational western thought, becomes as important as what is being said. Here Alter is interested in the translatability of meanings across media into different codes—from written to spoken text, French to English, sound to image, and how this "charges the [film's] images with surplus symbolic meaning".

The second film, *Cooperation of Parts*, 1987, is Eisenberg's most overtly autobiographical film. Made in 1987, it documents a trip he made to Europe in 1983. Starting in France he travels to Berlin, then to Warsaw and Radom, Poland, the birthplaces of his mother and father, and to Auschwitz and Dachau where they were interred during the Second

World War. In my essay on the film, "Fragments of an Inheritance: Contingences of History in *Cooperation of Parts*", I look at the ways Eisenberg explores the traumatic history of his own family as it is passed from one generation to another. Though the traumas of the parents were never directly experienced or fully explained, such trauma becomes internalized as incomplete or fragmented knowledge, merely gleaned or intuited, but which none-the-less has a structuring role in the lives of their children. Rather than creating a memoir that illustrates his family's catastrophe, from past to present, as in a work such as Art Spiegelman's *Maus*, *Cooperation of Parts* is a work that maintains his experience of incomplete and occluded knowledge. The film insists upon the experience of ephemerality, gaps—the limits of what can be represented and understood about the lives, not just of his survivor/parents, but more crucially his own. To do this Eisenberg creates a film of fragmented form, filled with jagged cuts, off kilter subjective camera work and open ended sequences bringing forth the experience of a haunted history not quite his own. In returning to the site of his parents' early life, Eisenberg questions his own identity in relation to post-war Europe, which in a counter-life might have been his own world. Through the lens of his parents' miraculous survival of the extermination camps, Eisenberg's film contemplates his very existence as a counter-narrative to the Nazi narrative of total Jewish annihilation. As I argue in the essay, "*Cooperation of Parts* suggests a different kind of formal and conceptual possibility for using cinema to interrogate a complex, multi-dimensional catastrophe of the proportions of the Shoah."

Persistence: Film in 24 absences/presences/prospects, 1997, is a portrait of the city of Berlin shot during the period of unification in 1991. In its transition, the city's modern history is revealed as a nodal point for much of twentieth century Europe's calamitous transitions, and is perhaps Eisenberg's most complex film. *Persistence* is an episodic work that turns the city into a into a kind of time machine as it moves back and forth between different historical moments and the events that constitute them. The film itself becomes a document of the city in the process of transformation, suspended between the demolition of a divided city, a signifier of Germany's total defeat in the Second World War and its renovation as the capital of the newly unified Germany. There are two essays that approach this third film in very different ways. In the first I invited Leora Auslander, an historian of European social history whose research focuses on the material culture in France and Germany, to write on the film as it relates to her own work on the twentieth century history of Berlin. In her essay, "Looking Across the Threshold: Persistence as Experiment in Time, Space, and Genre" she argues that in addition to being a work of cinematic art, *Persistence* is also a work of history. Her essay explores the ways that Eisenberg uses the film medium to expand the possibilities of historiography as a discipline. As Auslander writes, the film has much to teach historians about the specific problems it addresses—"evoking the contrast between the drama of historical cataclysm and the seeming normality of everyday life". In her close and sensitive reading of the film, she shows how *Persistence*, through a kind of poetics of time, through the textures of its images and juxtaposition of its sounds, through various kinds of documents and texts, is able to reframe traditional historical narratives of chronological unfoldings with more complex narratives of multiplicity and simultaneity. Auslander explores the ways the film medium itself activates other experiences of history not usually considered to be traditional parts of the historian's repertoire such as affects, sensations, and the dynamic experience of a world in flux. Like Eisenberg in *Persistence*, Auslander in her own research explores the absent presence of the once large, Jewish community in Berlin. In the essay she skillfully integrates her own research on the material artifacts— photographs, documents and personal objects that surround the deportations of Berlin's Jews during the war with Eisenberg's own visual explorations of the remnants of that community in the present. For Auslander, *Persistence* demonstrates that "attention to the situatedness of the historian and to the aesthetic and affective is not in contradiction with the historian's mission of conveying as close as she can come to the truth of the past, while being useful to the present".

The second essay on *Persistence* foregrounds German unification and the ways that historical break is made visible in the multiple forms of imagining the archive of German political and cultural history. In his essay, "The Persistence of the Archive: The Documentary Fictions of Daniel Eisenberg", cultural and literary theorist Scott Durham thinks about the ways the archive is created, recreated, and appropriated in the construction of new narratives for the history of an uncertain present. Taking off from Michel Foucault's remark that, in his excavations of the historical archive, he had never written anything but fictions, Durham begins with the film's account of an emblematic shift in the German political and cultural landscape since unification: the opening up of the archives of the Ministry for State Security, the Stasi, to its former subjects of surveillance, as part of the preservation of Stasi headquarters as a museum. Durham uses this to explore the ways in which Berlin itself appears in the film as a vast archive of documents and monuments, in which successive or contending archival fictions coexist. In *Persistence*, Eisenberg documents the process through which a newly unified Berlin attempts to refashion itself by reframing and reordering the elements of both its Communist and Nazi past. Durham shows how remainders of this earlier strata of German history with their monuments to Lenin and ruined of churches and synagogues can still be read within and alongside the new history as it is being rewritten, much in the same way that the discerning eye can detect the underwriting of a palimpsest. It is in this sense, as Durham writes, that *Persistence* becomes "an archive of archives, which at once constitutes a new archival space of its own and invites us to interrogate the relations between archival formations, and the narratives associated with them".

In *Something More Than Night*, 2003, Christa Blümlinger considers this contemplative "city symphony" of Chicago, filmed entirely at night. Unlike the city films of an earlier period, such as Vertov's *Man with a Movie Camera*, 1929, or Ruttmann's *Berlin: Symphony of a Great City*, 1927, which construct culturally specific urban spaces as dynamic, fast moving, and the embodiment of the utopian promise of a progressive future, Blümlinger reads the Chicago of *Something More than Night* as a paradigmatic contemporary post-war, post-industrial global urban heterotopia. The most formally structured of the four films, *Something More Than Night* is a series of 70 static shots that nocturnally explores the contemporary city as a series of modern non-spaces, which "despite its linear series of scenes, appears to have neither beginning nor end". With the camera often positioned outside looking in, we observe such non-spaces as airports, bus stations, and anonymous empty office buildings sometimes inhabited by equally anonymous figures such as janitors, security guards and the homeless. This is mixed with older remnants of an earlier incarnation of this once industrial American city such as an all night steel foundry or the lobby of one of Chicago's formerly grand public buildings. No longer an image of the future or the past, Blümlinger uses the film to meditate on these poetic images of an eternal present that characterizes our "supermodern" age... of solitary individuality, the temporary, fleeting, and ephemeral."

As the final film of the Postwar Quartet, *Something More Than Night* is the only one that is shot entirely in the United States and in Eisenberg's adopted home town. In the film however, home is a heterotopia constituted as neither here nor there, at once physical and imagined, familiar and strange. As with all of Eisenberg's films, home is a space of ephemeral layers reverberating between past and present and absence and presence, always producing something more than meets the eye.

Daniel Eisenberg himself has the last word in the volume with a short meditation upon his notion of postwar. He writes about the ways he sees the postwar inscribed in the landscape and in the simple acts of daily life. For Eisenberg, postwar is a state of being in the contemporary world, always suspended between the just before and just after—of catastrophe. He writes about this as a kind of peripheral, de-centered vision, which allows us to see the multiple historical contexts operating in the world, and in its images. It is in this Postwar that his films were made.

PERSISTENT DISPLACEMENTS
THE CITY FILMS OF DAN EISENBERG

Tom Gunning

Something More Than Night, Daniel Eisenberg, 2003

To know is to remember that you've seen. To see is to know without remembering. Thus painting is remembering the blackness.

Orhan Pamuk, *My Name is Red*

Although somewhat limited in number, the films of Daniel Eisenberg show a range of styles, never resting firmly in any single specific mode or genre. While clearly avant-garde films, their personal lyricism and enigmatic observation also recall (without ever conforming to) more familiar forms of non-fiction filmmaking: travel accounts, documentary chronicle, home movies, even the heritage (largely abandoned since the silent era) of the 'City Symphony' (a cinematic portrait of urban life). All these forms have resonance in his work, along with established modes of avant-garde filmmaking: the cinematic dairy; the family memoir: the found footage collage—even the fixed camera/long take structural film. Yet none of his films evoke any one of these forms exclusively, nor do these modes ever subordinate the variety of elements his films offer. Rather than genres or modes, his films offer a series of interwoven threads—more apparent when his films are seen in aggregate than singularly. These threads provide less themes of meaning (although they are strongly significant) than recurring obsessions, courses of imagery and issues that snake through his film, often functioning very differently from film to film, and evading any single purpose or principle.

FILMED HISTORY: PRESENTING THE PAST

... la forme d'une ville Change plus vite, hélas! que la coeur d'un mortel.
[... a city changes more quickly, alas, than a human's heart.]

Charles Baudelaire, *Le Cygne*

The thread that pulls this essay through this compact, but multifaceted, oeuvre evokes memory and history through images of places. *Persistence*, Eisenberg's film from 1997, thematizes this aspect most directly, with its meditation on (and even definition of) the issues of the monument and memory, its play of absence and presence. In this regard it is perhaps his most legible and profound film, even if at points seeming to sacrifice some of its resonance to the urge to render explicit. But *Persistence* also provides an approach to Eisenberg's other films, a moment of clarity (albeit certainly filled with ambiguity and complexity) that highlights aspects of his work as whole. Indeed the relation of Eisenberg's films one to another seems symphonic, with a series of shared themes and devices arrayed in different hierarchies from film to film. It was only after seeing *Persistence* that I experienced one of Eisenberg's earlier films *Displaced Person*, 1981, as presenting Hitler's entrance into Paris as a tour of monuments—the Eiffel Tower, the Arc de Triumphe, Notre Dame and La Madeleine.

In *Persistence* the theme of the monument, its dismantling and construction and its persistence and deterioration, takes the dominant role, while the film's role as a city symphony of Berlin remains secondary. But these themes could be said to change position in *Something More Than Night*, 2003, as the portrait of the city becomes the dominant mode, while the sense of architecture as monument and locus of memory persists as an overtone. The diary form so central in *Cooperation of Parts*, 1987, becomes one thread in *Persistence*, while the same film also recalls the collage of found footage that characterizes *Displaced Person* in its use of documentary (from archival footage from the U.S. Army Signal Corps to a film by Louis Lumière) and fiction films (Rossellini's *Germania Anno Zero*).

Left and opposite:
Displaced Person,
Daniel Eisenberg,
1981

Although strongly discursive in their use of language (spoken voice-over printed inter and subtitles delivering quotations and inscriptions), Eisenberg's film never explain themselves through these statements as much as they rub one against another, observing the friction engendered. But more than many films of the classical avant-garde, these films do ask that we read them, that we attempt to decipher their often fragmentary messages, engaging us in a hermeneutic effort, as archeologists of the twentieth century, historians of the present. As film viewers, Eisenberg asks us to remain alert to the medium's dialectical blend of the present with the past and vice versa. If the moving image, as some theorists have claimed, always exists in the present tense (we see events as they happen, not as events already completed), nonetheless the appearance of motion occurring before our eyes depends on the already existing inscription of images on the filmstrip. Film enacts a dialectic in which the past seems to live again, blossoming before our eyes.

But as it preserves (and perhaps even resurrects) a past moment, it also captures the flow of time, the process of decay. As Godard claimed, paraphrasing Cocteau, cinema shows us death at work. Eisenberg seizes upon the possibilities of cinema as a paradoxical historiographic machine, simultaneously overcoming and reinstating the course of time. Eisenberg approaches the cinematic image as always reaching beyond itself, into the past it seeks to recapture or remember, as well as into the future it anticipates. Intercutting his own footage with archival or historical footage, Eisenberg explores the historical dimension of both modes of film, his stance as cameraman participating in the same temporal paradoxes as incorporating found footage: the attempt to transfix the flight of time itself. History is for Eisenberg a personal quest, research into the enigmas and tragedies of his own genealogy. By linking personal memory to a memory that goes beyond the individual, Eisenberg's filmmaking widens to include his family (imagining the history of parents before one was born,) and the temporal shape of a city as the locus of human dwelling over time. As cinematic monuments, his films encounter the fragility and endurance of time in the most intangible of media, a form that imbricates time into its very perception.

Cooperation of Parts, Daniel Eisenberg, 1987

THE CINEMATIC MONUMENT

Tout les villes seraient pareilles si leur monuments ne les distinguaient pas.
[All cities would be the same, if their monuments didn't make it possible
to tell them apart.]

Alberto Cavalcanti, *Rien que les heures*

Traditionally, monuments memorialize: they enshrine and commemorate events. Persisting through ages as markers, often surviving only as ruins, they serve as tangible embodiments of memories. And yet monuments, with their connotations of magnitude and endurance seem conceived precisely to counter the fragile nature of human memory, its intangible invocation of something absent or past, the evanescent traces of a past held within a person's psyche. Monuments seek to shore up the fragility of human memory, endowing it with sterner material, as if rock, metal and cement could reinforce the delicate structure of the human brain and last through generations, surviving individual deaths. And yet monuments can also inspire a will to destruction, iconoclastic impulse that generally commemorated a change of regime. Think of the statue of the Czar torn apart in the opening of Eisenstein's *October*, Courbet's destruction of the Place Vendome Column during the Commune—and more recently—the disgraced monuments of the Soviet regime recorded in Laura Mulvey's documentary, the pulling down of the statue of Saddam Hussein in Baghdad, or the

Taliban's demolition of the statues of Buddha in Afghanistan. To build a monument seems to entail imagining its ruin and collapse as much as seeking to forestall it.

Cinema seems excluded from the ambitions of the monumental: an unstable chemical base, an insubstantial light-borne moving image when projected— evanescent, like shadow. Yet cinema too has a special relation to memory, partly through its filiation with photography. Oliver Wendell Holmes, writing during the American Civil War, described the threat the new medium of photography offered to the traditional monument: "Give us a few negatives of a thing worth seeing, taken from different points of view, and that is all we want of it. Pull it down or burn it up, if you please." In contrast to vast enduring monuments, one could claim that, for the last century and a half, the predominant image of memory has been provided primarily by the photograph. The photograph holds a relation to a specific moment; it preserves rather than defeats the progression of time. As the impress of a moment (Bazin called photography a "light mould"), the photograph seems the perfect exteriorization of the impression of memory, the retention of an image of a specific time. The monument speaks of what endures, of the *longue durée* of time; the photograph speaks of the transient, even the instantaneous, the contingent and the momentary. Between the monument and the photograph runs the gamut of memory.

In his dialogue the *Phaedrus*, Plato described the dialectic between living memory and its exteriorization. Telling a myth of the origin of writing by the Egyptian God Thoth, he describes the Egyptian King Ammon rejecting Thoth's claim that the art of writing will

Demolition of a Wall, August and Louis Lumière, 1895, in *Persistence*, Daniel Eisenberg, 2007

improve man's memory. Instead, Ammon claims, writing will "implant forgetfulness in their soul. They will cease to exercise memory because they rely on that which is written, recalling things to remembrance no longer from within themselves, but by means of external marks."[1] We could make the same claim about photographs: that they have replaced internal recall with external images. How many of us know if we remember a childhood pet, our parents when young, or the features of a lost friend, or simply remember a photograph we have of them? Home movies carry the same tumble of the promise of preservation with the threat of amnesia, as projected images seem to dislodge our memories.

But rather than rekindling those lost images, plugging in the gaps in the fabric of memories and the erasures of history, Eisenberg's films explore the process of creating blanks as much as filling them. Eisenberg's camera examines the places in his film for what is no longer there, for what has been destroyed or forgotten. But forgetting is never so simple. It leaves traces powerful in themselves, not simply clues to what once was, but signs of the violence that engenders history. Thus for Eisenberg, the photographic nature of the moving image becomes a vehicle not only for the recording of the past, for memory as retention, but of the gaps left in the portrayal of history, what has been concealed, what has remained unknown and what exceeds our vision. The past in Eisenberg's films is not only subject to construction and destruction, but to reconstruction as well as deconstruction. While monuments may slowly crumble or be violently pulled down, the preservation of human memory may be best guaranteed by stories, by the insubstantial nature of shared language

Persistence

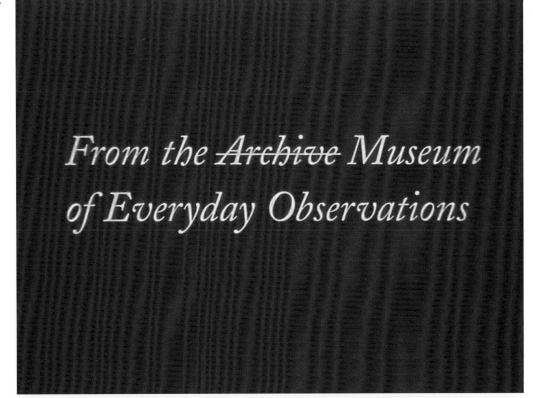

and telling. If memory traces can be thought of as individual psychic facts, stories are social practices, exchanged between people. Monuments may lose their meaning, their inscriptions effaced or rendered untranslatable, but stories endure even as they transform, shedding meanings and gaining new significances, becoming legends instead of facts. Films can be vehicles for stories, clothing them in images and dramatic reconstructions, interweaving facts and stories, legends and history. But Eisenberg's films rarely tell a story as much as they seem to seek one out, an elusive tale that remains fragmentary, inconsistent and ultimately, untold.

The American avant-garde cinema deviated from the path of storytelling, at least as it became standardized by the modern world's most powerful storyteller, the Hollywood movie, and sought inspiration in what founding figure Maya Deren called the "vertical attack", the plumbing of a moment for its emotional resonance or significance rather than furthering the forward thrust of narrative action. Plunging or ascending, the avant-garde filmmaker could employ symbolic or ritual action, or as Stan Brakhage put it, allow the walls of narrative to collapse completely and make a film directly from "eye-sources", from the lyrical encounter of filmmaker, camera and world. Seeking an intensity of experience pushed avant-garde filmmakers toward portraying the immediacy of overwhelming ecstasy or trauma, liberated from the concatenation of time that Deren characterized as the horizontal development. Dreams and fantasy, the transcendence of time offered by ritual, or the mythic time of *illo tempore* obsessed the first generation of the American avant-garde cinema. Although intensely aware of the dialectics of metaphor and signification, of the elusive nature of all allusion to

Left and opposite:
Displaced Person

these transcendent realms, and often filled with ironic reflection on the inadequacies of representation, nonetheless these filmmakers envisioned a richly visionary cinema, suffused with saturated color, complex editing, and rapid motion.

While one should avoid drawing too sharp distinctions between periods of style, I believe a different tone emerged in certain American avant-garde films in the 1960s and the following decades. Although the realms of ecstasy and metaphor remain key references, these films project a sense of time passing as much as ecstatic escape and of historical exile, as much as personal alienation. In extremely unique and very different ways, the films of Ken Jacobs, Ernie Gehr and Jonas Mekas evoked a new sense of history and loss. The film image itself becomes the repository of history (Gehr's and Jacobs' use of found and archival footage, explored not simply as historical document, but as artifact of the passage of time itself), while specific films reference the experience of displacement and extermination caused by the Second World War (Gehr's *Signal: Germany on the Air*; Jacobs' *Urban Peasants* and *The Alps and the Jews*; Mekas' *Reminiscences of a Journey to Lithuania* to offer obvious examples). This is a cinema of loss and memory, of history and mourning. Beyond immediacy these filmmakers descended into the materials of history (both the vast archive of cinema itself to the resources of personal memory) to find a story that went beyond the visionary cycles of inspiration and disillusion or sexual identity, and sought the riddle of the self in the nature of the social and its betrayals.

In this tradition Eisenberg, like many younger filmmakers in the 70s and 80s, approached the cinematic image as a material and historical trace, exploring the possibilities

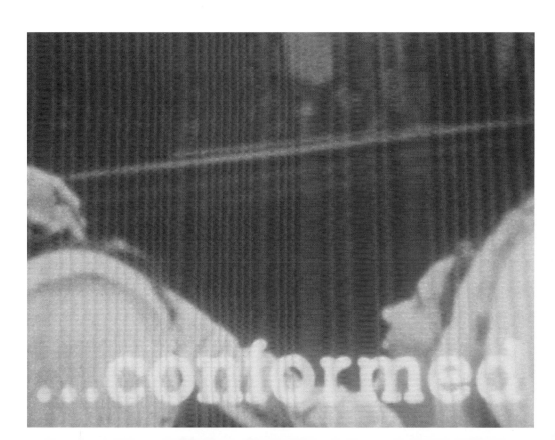

Left and opposite:
Persistence

of found and archival footage. *Displaced Person* uses historical footage of Hitler's entrance into Paris, but the imagery does not simply serve as historical reference. Originally shot for Nazi newsreels, Eisenberg scavenged the footage from an exhibition print of Marcel Ophüls' documentary *The Sorrow and the Pity*, so that subtitles commenting on Hitler's limited knowledge of French culture overlay the scenes. That the film print itself had a history, that the footage of Hitler had been recycled and redefined first by Ophüls and then by Eisenberg himself exemplifies film's historical and material nature. Seeing the footage of Hitler visiting La Madeleine in Ophüls' film, Eisenberg had realized he, as tourist in Paris, had also stood where Hitler once stood. Thus the monument marks a point where successive times intersect, where one viewpoint can encounter another one existing in a different time, but taking in the same place. In *Displaced Person* Eisenberg does not simply recycle the original footage of Hitler, but attempts to digest it, to scrutinize and interrogate it. His manipulation of the footage with an optical printer, serves partly to abstract its forms through exaggerated contrast and repetition.

But more than formal transformation, the film undertakes a cross examination of the moving image. Again and again instead of using cinema as a metaphor for vision, Eisenberg seems to subject the film image to a visual probing, even to torment it, as if hoping it can yield up the secrets of the past and of history. In *Persistence*, Eisenberg uses his camera as a dissecting tool on the buildings of Berlin, revealing the scars and traces of history they retain in their surfaces. Architecture like film shows signs of use, the pockmarks of violence, and the failed attempts at concealment.

Interrogated in this manner, monuments become less tributes to heroic triumphs, than evidence of guilt, unconsciously betraying other motives as their facade slips, revealing crime scenes. Although Eisenberg does not use the cinematic technique of superimposition, it stands as a metaphor for the sense of history discovered in his films. Nearly every image seems to superimpose another view of this same site, another time when other eyes glimpsed it, with other purposes and other cares. Thus *Persistence*, searches buildings for the signs of other buildings, probing into hallways and doorways as if they held shadows of other lives.

A superimposition might betray this method by literalizing it, for it is the sense of the absent revealed through their present traces, even attempts at effacement, that Eisenberg wishes to reveal. His cinema renders the invisible palpable through the resonance of place and history, rather than special effects. Sound in interaction with image often takes on this role of evocation. In *Persistence* Eisenberg occasionally creates sound effects to accompany archival footage not, as in a television documentary, in order to make it seem more present, but precisely to generate an impossible ghostly echo. Eisenberg occasionally manages a seeming match between sound and image, only then to move them further apart, so that we sense their increasing non-congruence. Thus *Cooperation of Parts* opens with a voice-over that seems to describe the scene we watch, people gathered at a train station. But then we notice discrepancies in description and we realize not only that the voice-over is not describing this scene (instead referring to an unseen photograph), but that this mismatch expresses the mission of the film: the desire of the child to imagine his parents' past, to match up stories and images, memories and fictions that don't seem to fit—to critique and recreate history.

Top: Eisenberg family
photographs, 1949

Bottom: *Cooperation
of Parts*

THE WIND FROM PARADISE

Dieu annonce qu'il a l'intention de monter un cinéma et qu'il a les plus beaux films de guerre. [God announces that he intends to open a movie theater, and that he has the greatest war movies ever made.]

Blaise Cendrars, *The End of the World as Filmed by the Angel Notre Dame*

The holocaust and its personal effect on his family (his parents being survivors of the camps in Germany and the U.S.S.R.) play a key role in Eisenberg's cinema. The critical work undertaken recently on the representation of the *Shoah* and of trauma provides a rich background for his work. Although this context forms a horizon for my discussion of his films, I will not focus on it directly. Such personal tragedy opens more broadly onto the horror of history, and Eisenberg seems guided here by Walter Benjamin's image of the Angel of History. *Persistence* begins with references to this angel, whom Benjamin, inspired by a drawing by Paul Klee, describes as, "an angel who seems about to move away from something he stares at". Benjamin describes the angel's gaze as: "turned toward the past".

Where a chain of events appear before us, he sees one single catastrophe, which keeps piling wreckage upon wreckage and hurls it at his feet. The angel would like to stay, awaken the dead, and make whole what has been smashed. But the storm is blowing from Paradise and has got caught in his wings; it so strong that the angel can no longer close them. This storm drives him irresistibly into the future, to which his back is turned, while the pile of debris before him grows towards the sky. What we call progress is this storm.[2]

Eisenberg's imagery provides a cinematic translation of the passage. We see an extraordinary shot of the angel (actually a winged figure of Victory) on top of the Victory column in Berlin. This sublime shot is heavily mediated cinematically: taken most likely from a moving car with a telephoto lens and optically processed, the figure appears as a progressively darker silhouette seeming to sail along with the moving camera, glimpsed through moving tree branches. The optical ambiguity of the shot endows the monument

Left to right: Three angels—*Angelus Novus*, Paul Klee, 1920, copyright the Israel Museum, Jerusalem, photograph by David Harris, copyright DACS 2010; Walter Benjamin portrait, bpk/Germaine Krull; drawing by Fernand Léger from the book *The End of the World as Filmed by the Angel Notre Dame* by Blaise Cendrars,1919

with an uncanny motion, so that it flies through the branches that eventually eclipse it like some primal fury. Eisenberg cuts from this apparently airborne figure to aerial shots of Berlin in ruins after the Second World War, the skeletons of buildings huddled below in seemingly endless panoramas of destruction. The angle of view and the continuation of motion transform this archival footage into the angel's viewpoint cast onto the accumulation of disasters below. These shots give way seamlessly to a high angle shot of Edmund, the young boy protagonist of Rossellini's Germania Anno Zero, running through these same ruined streets. In this first sequence, the image of the angel of history unites personal, archival and fictional modes of the filmmaking, linking widely separate periods of history (footage shot by Eisenberg, presumably in the 80s with images from the post-war era; Germany's military victories in the 1870s celebrated by the monument matched with images of its defeat in 1945).

Eisenberg images the angel of history as the power of cinema, creating an apocalyptic cinematic angel of history that recalls Blaise Cendrars poem from the 1920's (illustrated by Fernand Léger) *The End of the World as Filmed by the Angel Notre Dame*. Rather than a winged victory we see an exterminating angel, moving through the heavens over Berlin. Berlin exists as a city of disgraced monuments, eras of successive regime changes creating a palimpsest of twentieth century ideology, the actual point where West split from East, a city with its own interior border, the Wall, graffiti-ridden in one of Eisenberg's films (*Cooperation of Parts*) and scheduled to disappear in another (*Persistence*).

Persistence

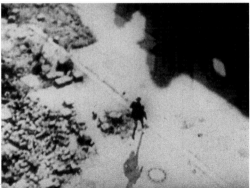

Left and bottom: *Persistence*

Right: *Klosterruine Eldena*, Caspar David Friederich, 1825, oil on canvas, 35 x 49 cm, Berlin, Nationalgalerie

But if this flying cinematic angel could be seen as a source of destruction and retribution from the skies, Eisenberg appears more involved in imagining its view onto the disasters of history. The wind blows the angel backwards into a future he cannot see, while his eyes remain transfixed by the past accumulating before him. Withdrawing from all this, he cannot foreswear his role as witness. The soundtrack early in *Persistence* describes the most reified forms of such witnessing: history as the drawing up and balancing of accounts, witnessing as a protocol of surveillance and spying. The spoken commentary dissects these procedures into repeatable techniques even as the images show perhaps the most ecstatic portrayal of beholding in Western art, the enraptured witnesses in the paintings of Caspar David Freidrich.

The filmmaker stands before these images in contemplation, as if wondering if such a mode of vision can be given to the camera, better designed perhaps for gathering evidence and drawing up accounts.

Persistence

ANTICIPATION OF THE NIGHT

Birg dich tief in das Auge der Nacht, Daß dein Tag nachtdunkeltrage.
[Shelter yourself deep in the eye of night so your day wears the
nocturnal darkness.]
Else Lasker-Schüller, *The Voices of Eden*

Seventeenth century French writer, Rene-Alain Le Sage reworked the Jewish arch-
demon Asmodeus into a mischievous if sinister figure who has the ability to peer
through roofs and see the concealed sins occurring within, a power perhaps also
given to the avenging angel flying over Berlin at the opening of *Persistence*. But
what if the walls of buildings themselves were made of glass, if, paradoxically, the
very transparency of a modern society became its ultimate technique of opacity?
Eisenberg's most recently completed film *Something More Than Night* (2003) may
seem to abandon the themes of history and interrogation so evident in the films that
revolve around Europe and the holocaust. Filmed entirely at night in Eisenberg's
current home city, Chicago, the film avoids the signs of personal presence found
in so many of his other films: the handheld camera, the voice-over and personal
narratives, the research into family history. But, as in so much of his work, I believe
the film represents less a transition in style, than another arrangement of his basic
themes. The issue of place and edifice remains central to this film, if approached in
a new manner.

Historical connections, of course, exist between Chicago and the European sites
featured in Eisenberg's other films. Berlin of the 20s looked to Chicago (more
than New York) for the image of the modern metropolis, and the city appears in
phantasmagoric form in the early plays of Bertolt Brecht. German modernist
architects saw Chicago as the home of a new mode of urban life. Eric Mendelsohn's
extraordinary Schocken department stores clearly borrowed elements from Louis
Sullivan's design for Mayer's Department Store that Mendelsohn had admired during

Left: Schocken
Department Store in
Stuttgart, 1928, copyright
Landesmedienzentrum
BW

Right: Schlesinger and
Mayer Department Store,
Chicago, Louis Sullivan,
1899, courtesy of the
Frances Loeb Library,
Harvard Graduate School
of Design

Something More
Than Night

a trip to Chicago. Mendelsohn also submitted a utopian plan for a skyscraper
made of glass to the 1922 competition for the Chicago Tribune Tower (alas, turned
down). When the Bauhaus was driven out of Germany by the Nazis, it found a home
in Chicago, as did the last director of the Bauhaus in Germany, Mies van der Rohe,
some of whose buildings are seen in *Something More Than Night*. Beyond these
artistic connections, Chicago is traditionally the American city of immigrants and
migrants, from the influx of immigrants from Eastern and Northern Europe at
the end of the nineteenth century on (Chicago has the largest Polish population of
any city after Warsaw), the waves of Mexican workers that flocked to Chicago area
factories during Second World War, and the Great Migration of southern blacks
during the 20s, all these transplanted citizens make Chicago a city of diversity
and transformation.

Something More Than Night reflects this aspect of the city, from the variety of workers
we see and hear as the undertake their nocturnal tasks, to the film's recurring image
of Chicago as transition point, a way station in a constant and unending process of
transportation; bus stations, freeways, train stations and airports crowd the film.
More perhaps than a city of monuments, Eisenberg sees Chicago as a waiting room,
a space between destinations.

The film initially seems to invert the most famous of city symphonies, Walter
Ruttmann's *Berlin, die Symphonie der Grossstadt* from 1927. Ruttmann's film
begins at dawn as workers stream into Berlin to begin their workday; Eisenberg
begins at night with images of people leaving offices and work. But this inversion
poses more of a tease than a structure for the film. As Eisenberg shows, in the
modern city works never stops, and his film never follows the clear temporal
progression that pilots Ruttmann thorough the city and its diurnal round. Although
the film carries an important sense of accumulation, it avoids the montage that
drives Ruttmann's film with a cinematic equivalent of urban tempo. Instead of
counting down the hours towards dawn, night appears as a permanent state,
or at least a static one, pervasive, as time in Eisenberg's film reflects duration
rather than acceleration, recycling the fixed framing and long takes of the structural
films of the 70s into a new context. These lengthy, rarely moving shots project
the time of waiting, the human experience of time that Heidegger describes as
"stretching along", through the film.

*Berlin: Symphony of
a Great City*, Walter
Ruttmann, 1927

*Something More
Than Night*

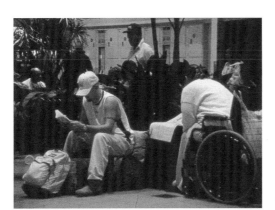

Night arches over this film, defining its imagery and its tone. While night signifies darkness, a barrier to vision that depends on light, the modern city re-defines itself through its artificial daylight, which illuminates and, to use Wolfgang Schivelbusch's lovely phrase, "disenchants the night".

The modern city (and architecture in Chicago and Berlin in the early twentieth century were beacons in this regard) transforms night with a series of optical devices, light most obviously, but also glass. The lit shop window created a spectacle at night in which the spell of the commodity united with the effect of illumination to create a scenography of desire. Eisenberg shows the display of goods only briefly, but peering into a brightly lit quadrilateral window or doorway dominates the film. A large pane of glass (whose manufacture transformed modern architecture) allows vision to enter, but still maintains a barrier.

The film opens staring like a voyeur into the space of offices, watching silent conversations and gestural dramas of departure. Peering in from the outside, the composition sets an opening stance for the film that clearly separates the seer from the seen, portioning out very different spaces and roles. For the most part sound comes from the seer's side of the glass (often referring to off-screen unseen events), while the figures glimpsed through windows become actors in a silent film, communicating to us through gestures and pantomime. The seer figured by the camera remains invisible, yet authoritative, the author of the view we share.

Berlin: Symphony of a Great City

The urban spectator first appeared in the figure that Walter Benjamin described as the *flâneur*, the idler who strolls through streets and squares, observing the panorama of urban characters and scenes around him. The *flâneur* moved on the level of the world he observes, possessing none of the overview that Asmodeus or the angel of history claim. But the observer in *Something More Than Night* differs from both these viewpoints. He gazes into the world, but generally from outside (not only windows, but doorways and corridor separate him from the scene of his observation). He is an outsider who stares at what unfolds before him. Rather than a flâneur, he seems a stalker, that unseen threat that observes the vulnerable from the outside.

The scenography of the contemporary slasher films may seem out of place in a film whose leisurely pace hardly evokes a genre based in bloodbaths and chases. But as anodyne as the action in this film seems, a deeper darkness seeps into the frame. The title itself evokes genre cinema, the film noir, not only by its allusion to a famous quote from hard-boiled author Raymond Chandler, "the streets were dark with *Something More Than Night*", but through the echoes it stirs from films noir: *Naked City* which opens with an description of New York City at night, the odyssey of Richard Widmark through the dark alleys of London in *Night and the City*, or the little known noir set in Chicago *The City that Never Sleeps*. Certainly on one level such comparisons are ironic; instead of murders and fleeing gangster, Eisenberg discovers everyday (or everynight) occurrences, yet what we see is less a sense of community (even when people gather together, the silence and the darkness surrounding them creates a sense of isolation) than of frames defined by artificial

Something More Than Night

light, sheltering folk from something more than darkness. (Hopper's unfortunately overexposed masterpiece *Nighthawks* provides another iconic guide for the film.)

As P. Adams Sitney has taught us, a key moment in the history of the American avant-garde film occurred with Brakhage's turn from the tradition of symbolist and expressionist influenced psychodrama to the immediacy of the lyrical mode in his watershed film *Anticipation of the Night* in 1958. As I mentioned earlier, Brakhage described this experience as the collapse of the walls of a structure he could no longer inhabit. And what lies beyond the walls? "When those walls fell, it seemed as if there were nothing but night out there and I then thought of all my life as being in anticipation of that night."[3] For Brakhage that night cast the shadow of the hanged man, of suicide, which he refers to (and nearly literally enacted) at the end of his film. The darkness of Brakhage's film takes the shape of a projection of self and its annihilation. The isolation felt in *Something More Than Night* is never singular and avoids personal drama. The city itself is lonely. Eisenberg's earlier city films tried to wrest some understanding of the past from the monuments and ruins he confronted. In this film the places are obscure, shrouded in a darkness. Whereas Ruttmann's Berlin seems to race through its daily round, Chicago seems stranded in an endless night. Clocks appear in some shots, but chart no progress. People ply their trades, but even the factory workers, food vendors, waitresses and maintenance men seem to be waiting for the night to end, as surely as the men who sleep in railway stations as children play video games (propelling a animated racing car that speeds down a street but never can leave the frame of the monitor). The camera here seems less to interrogate the images before it than, to wait for them to unfold in their own

*Something More
Than Night*

time. If one senses a recurrent separation between the camera/observer and the city it watches in this film, nonetheless they are united in the act of waiting. This night does not project itself as Eisenberg's personal vision. It is a time and space he shares with others, a space of waiting. Rather than scrutinizing or even stalking, the camera in *Something More Than Night* watches. Watches and waits. One recalls the verses from the Book of Isaiah:

Watchman, what of the Night? Watchman what of the night? The watchman said, the morning cometh and also the night; if ye will inquire, inquire ye: return, come.
Isaiah, 21/11, 12

Writing in Weimar Germany in 1922, Siegfried Kracauer, major film theorist and historian and friend and interlocutor of Walter Benjamin, described an alternative to those who responded to the crisis of the modern world by embracing some form of faith, whether religious or political. Avoiding as well simple skepticism, Kracauer described a third possibility: "those who wait." This waiting, Kracauer urged, should contain no passivity or idleness, but remain an openness, "a tense activity."[4] Eisenberg knows as much as anyone, that a deadly fate overtook so many of those who waited. But this fact does not reduce their courage or insight. In early twentieth-first century America, one wonders what darkness more than night we are dwelling in, and how long it will last. Watch. Wait. Return.

Nighthawks,
Edward Hopper, 1942,
detail, oil on canvas,
84.1 x 152.4 cm,
Friends of American
Art Collection, 1942.51,
The Art Institute
of Chicago

*Berlin: Symphony
of a Great City*

*Cooperation
of Parts*

KIDS ON A BIKE

Raymond Bellour

You never choose your moments. They come and go: sometimes sifted through the screen of memory's chance-ridden paths, other times in response to the desire to take inventory, to prove a point, or to reactivate a more or less past shock so that it might be shared. There are so many such moments, so many shots in so many films. So many emotions attach to shots like these; they are almost unknown until a choice magnetizes them, which suddenly breaths a new and quasi-excessive life into them, making them exemplary. These moments choose you, perhaps have already chosen you, before you could ever even think of making them the possible motif of an argument. This is why no justification for them is necessary, even if the many reasons behind an argument can make them seem to fall neatly into the place a given criterion assigns to them. But they will only ever correspond to that place halfway, always remaining that much less or that much more than the view into whose service they have been drafted—a view that could never reduce their excess vitality. Their resonance will always be too vast and never fully known. Most often, this resonance remains within the limits of an idea that tears a specific shot from the film and returns it altered by its insistence on both using and serving it, while running the risk of treating the shot as if it were eternal. Occasionally, the resonance penetrates even further, into the realm of a personal intimacy so immediate that it may take time for it to become clear and to find its proper place in the temporality of individual memory which, for itself, can only be conceived of as overwhelming and insane.

And so, at the very beginning of Daniel Eisenberg's *Displaced Person,* 1981, we have two children passing by on a bike. At first, they pass by four separate times in a block of almost ten seconds, thus allowing very little time for each one of these identical passages. Only one passing-by would have created the shock of an ellipse, the enigma of a striking image gone before it can be recorded by the body's mind. Yet the fact that this very image, this one brief shot, is taken up four different times is as disconcerting as it is reassuring. Like breathing starting again, without ever fully returning. The camera, like the bike, glides by to fall into the strange off-screen space that then becomes the next beginning of the very same shot. The end of the last of these four shots, a little longer than the previous three, gives the bike time to leave the screen definitively; a shot with no relation to it whatsoever takes over the screen.[1]

At first, the bike is entirely contained within the frame: the bottom of the front wheel touches the edge of the image. At the end, in the first three shots, you can only barely make out the top of the back wheel. The older child, an adolescent, is sitting on the seat and pedaling; he is wearing a dark pair of pants and a dark shirt with its sleeves rolled up. The younger, in black pants and a white shirt, is sitting sideways on the frame; in his right hand he holds a badminton racquet that is raised at the beginning,

Displaced Person,
Daniel Eisenberg, 1981

and which, with a mechanical gesture, he will lower as the bike moves forward. The older child looks straight ahead, as someone driving has a tendency to do; but his face, half way through the shot, turns toward us. It's at this point that his brother—they look so much alike we can only imagine that's who it is—also turns around and the two faces stare at us together. Otherwise, both at the beginning and especially at the end of the shot, the younger child is staring off to his right and to our left, at a point that will remain imaginary and contributes to magnifying the event's attendant anxiety. Perhaps, as the movements continue, the two children will speak to one another. At the back of the frame, we can see, all too quickly at first, the back of a car, and then a car with an open trunk in front of which a man stands, then vague silhouettes that can barely be made out against their background of uncertain forms, perhaps stores, shops, and displays.

I do not know if the disturbance incited by this sequence of similar shots is heightened by the insistent tone of the *adagio con motto* of Beethoven's third "*Razumovski Quartet*. It may also be related to the subject matter of this ten minute experimental film that uses archival images of the only trip Hitler made to Paris in June 1940. The discovery of this moment opened up a world of primordial associations for the filmmaker.[2] But I will never be able to know this with any certainty since, for no obvious reason, these shots return twice: once at the first third and again at the second third of the film. By virtue of the fact that the sequence is repeated, it becomes charged with all that the film reveals. The second series has the shot return eight identical times, except that the first is buried in a black-out that separates it from the seven others for a brief moment; the third series is only repeated three times. This reiteration is not surprising in a film that is orchestrated by the return and rhyming effects of its elements. Because its subject matter is very similar, one notes in particular another shot of a bike: this time a young girl is perched on top of a machine far too large for her and is followed by another girl. This fixed-camera shot also returns within a tighter frame; it, too, is repeated four times. But for me, its effect has no common measure with the boys on the bike. It matters very little that, as I have since learned, the two and a half second shot comes from an American archive and was taken before the war. For me, it drives us straight into the war.

I don't really see a scene, but I do recall knowledge mixed with a feeling. In Lyon, during the Occupation, my parents had bought a two-seated bicycle to replace the car that was parked in a garage for lack of fuel. They used it in particular for scouring the countryside in search of black market products. If I remember correctly, they sometimes took me along and sat me in a basket at the back of the bike. A lot separates these two images, and one of them is actually not even an image. Perhaps it's simply the effect of the movement of any bike as it glides by, whether you are looking from the bike or at it. An uncanny movement of a ghost-image that the camera's gliding pan emphasizes. [Mouvement de filage, que le glissement de la caméra soutient.] The unknown body's memory. I know that the intensity my eyes see in the shot as reconfigured by Daniel Eisenberg comes from its having given rise to the affect of a memory that, without this chance encounter, would have never existed. And the power of the film's use of the repetition of these few frames is entirely crucial to this sense. Its power is not so much to be found in the fact that the figure is anchored in our memory by virtue of returning two more times, but in the effect it produces each time. It portrays movement that comes back from its end to its

beginning and thus begs our excessive attention, asking us to retain it in some way, to immobilize it, even though, with an irrepressible fatalism, it always moves onward too quickly; its coming and its going, as it were, refuse any attempt to grasp them, thus transforming this recurring movement into a pure effect of time. A stand-still within movement, or rather, movement at a stand-still. This tension is the source of a kind of internal image of the body opening up to possible recollection.

Of course, this is obliterated by all the film unveils. Those cutting images of Hitler visiting Paris. And especially those images of a train, of Hitler arriving and then leaving, waving from the window, cheered on by bodies, by women's bodies whose excitement responds to the train's movement. Images that return and return again as a way of underlining their haunting nature. Each image is more or less uncertain, and often rendered even more ghostly by the way the filmmaker has rephotographed them, causing each to decay in his attempt to approach them. There is one body in particular, a woman's body, lifting an arm, shaking her hand, taken away by her run all the way to the end of the platform where she seems to freeze in a posture of obscene desire. So that she alone becomes a screen, the figure, for impossible memory. The haircut, the corsage, the skirt, an indefinable something all make this look like a picture hidden away in a family photo album. Overwhelming memory. Above all, oscillating through so many figurative levels, from the clearest to the most abstract, there are also all those images of trains that recur throughout a film grounded in its initial theme of the journey—in such a way that the now unavoidable identity of the death trains and the train as an intermittent image of the many components of the cinematic apparatus is reinforced. In *Displaced Person*, all of these elements heighten the affect embodied by the repeated shot of boys on a bike.

They also attest to the difficulty of isolating one figure, one shot, or one group of shots from the rest of the film. Yet this is how both our senses and our memory work: through distinct shocks that seem to tear themselves from their context, but for that very reason nourish it, and find themselves affected by it in return. The banality of this experience characteristic of the time arts, and especially of film, has led it to be too often overlooked. Most of the time, a desire to argue a point prevails and either isolates the figure, in the name of a given shot, or else seizes it within a network that is thought to exemplify one logic if not the logic of a film. In a way, though, and however occasionally precise and powerful its effects may be, a given figure will always float and remain unresolved, drifting according to the developments of its unfolding body. And this floating is also its strength.

Translated by Will Bishop.

SOUND SCORES
MUSICAL ARMATURE
IN *DISPLACED PERSON*

Nora M. Alter

Music, I maintain, must in sound film never be the accompaniment.
It must retain its own line.
VI Pudovkin

Music is something that carries no traces, that cannot be marked, and that has
no scars. It remains untouched by history, by events, by horror.
Michel Chion

There is no appropriate language for witnessing. Where testimony has to
express the experience of the inhuman, it naturally finds an already constituted
language of becoming inhuman, of an identity between human sentiments and
non-human movements. It is a language whereby aesthetic fiction is opposed
to representative fiction.
Jacques Rancière

A myth coded in sounds instead of words, the musical work furnishes a grid
of signification, a matrix of relationships which filters and organizes lived
experience; it substitutes for experience and produces the pleasurable illusion
that contradictions can be overcome, and difficulties resolved.
Claude Lévi-Strauss

Creativity is not so much in finding new materials, but in the reconstruction
of materials that already exist.
Umberto Eco

The haunting strains of a violin playing Beethoven's *String Quartet #9, Opus 59 in C major #3*, 1808, serve to guide the viewer through Daniel Eisenberg's *Displaced Person*, 1981. Referred to as the "Rasumovsky" Quartets, the music selected by Eisenberg for his soundtrack is from the second movement of the third of three Beethoven compositions commissioned by the Russian Count Andreas Kyrillovich Rasumovsky, Russian Ambassador to Vienna and Beethoven's patron during the first decade of the nineteenth century. In Eisenberg's film this remarkable piece is played in its entirety, approximately ten minutes, equaling the length of the film. This is striking indeed since it is the only component on both the audio and visual track that is not a fragment, but exists in its totality.

The first in a cycle of three films which examine history and memory, *Displaced Person* is a compilation film comprised entirely of found footage that Eisenberg combines and recombines in multiple variations. Some of the material comes from Marcel Ophüls' *The Sorrow and the Pity*, 1970, other sequences are from the *Deutsches Wochenschau* of June 25, 1940, that recorded Hitler's dawn visit to Paris that same year, and still others from American newsreels. The visual images, without any matched original soundtrack, recur in a complex structure that at once reinscribes them historically while concomitantly wrenching them out of their original context. According to Eisenberg, the impetus to make the film suddenly occurred when he saw the *Wochenschau* footage of Hitler walking up the steps of La Madeleine in Paris:

I realized that I too had stood in that same spot, and read the inscription on the building and sat down there. To consider the fact that during my first trip to Europe, in my head; it was a revelation of some kind. Space and time seemed to collapse into one. And I realized, aside from the fact that his political program and history had in fact created my very being, because my parents met in Dachau after the war, there we were crossing paths.[1]

Proust's now infamous "Madeleine" biscuit, the smell or taste of which unleashed memories of a lost time, has transformed into an equally powerful mnemonic device as an architectural structure of La Madeleine. In both instances, the linguistic signifier of the proper name "Madeleine", whether a cake or a church, serves as a memory trigger. The "Madeleine" brings back a past time, a history, and forces it into the present day consciousness. The monument has drawn very different viewers—a conquering dictator from across the Rhine and an artist filmmaker from across the Atlantic. The powerful magnetism of La Madeleine attracts two radically different visitors. La Madeleine is a cultural touchstone. Visitors who gaze upon the stone edifice bring with them myriad and disparate histories. In a similar way, the placement of *Opus 59* in *Displaced Person* functions as an acoustic touchstone.

Hitler ascending La Madeleine is just one of many fragments out of which *Displaced Person* is composed. Often interspersed with several seconds of black leader, the fragments are repeated numerous times in different arrangements and combinations. Clips from the *Wochenschau* footage show Hitler visiting the Eiffel Tower, L'Arche de Triumphe, and Notre Dame; while another set of images dating from approximately the same time reveal Hitler on a train pulling away from a crowded station as the

Displaced Person,
Daniel Eisenberg, 1981

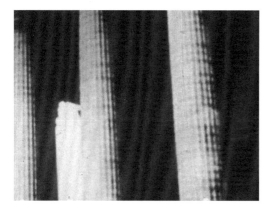

camera tracks a Red Cross nurse ecstatically racing after him. A different sequence depicts two young clean-cut boys who ride towards the camera on their shared bike, and in another, a child washes a doll, while elsewhere children play in a German town, and on a formal stage a dance sequence is recorded. The use of another's footage in compilation films is similar to the practice of quotation. Eisenberg chooses these quotes carefully seemingly aware of Walter Benjamin's dictum that "to write history... means to quote history", but at the same time the quotation takes the original document out of its historical context.[2]

Taken from varied and multiple sources, the viewer is not informed of the national origins or motivations behind the initial production of these clips. What do we make of these different pieces, these incomplete shards and fragments? One explanation is that within aesthetic production, principles of montage, collage and pastiche have elevated the fragment to a new status in the twentieth century. Eisenberg taps into this tradition as he explains that fragments have "been part of art-making and esthetics for a long time in this century.... Fragments sometime have a way of reflecting or breaking things apart." In addition, fragmentation corresponds with an essayistic mode of thought that for Theodor Adorno emerges in a shattered world that "thinks in fragments... and finds unity in and through the breaks and not by glossing them over".[3] This same fractured way of thinking is then translated into essay films—audio-visual productions that are neither documentaries nor fictional works but rather present themselves as philosophical or aesthetic mediations.[4] What remains to be seen is whether we are able to follow the suggestion of the voice-over on the soundtrack of *Displaced Person* and "find an order behind this apparent disorder".

The fragments are not as haphazard as they appear; one common thread is that all were made in the late 1930s and the early 1940s just before and during the Second World War. As Mary Ann Doane observes, extending Siegfried Kracauer's temporal theory of photography, "film makes visible not a knowledge of the original but a certain passing temporal configuration".[5] Their visual resemblance all points to the past. This shared time period coupled with Eisenberg's careful montage, demands that connections be drawn. The reorganization of the sequences serves to redirect and reorient our relation to the sounds and images, thereby uncovering embedded meanings. Eisenberg manipulates the images with the aid of an optical printer. Thus, for instance, in the sequence with the boys on the bicycle, their bike appears to move against a stationary background, while at other times the opposite occurs. The effect is to arrest history and the development of the characters. The boys' movement across the screen, abruptly interrupted, is constantly repeated and replayed. Not allowed to develop, the progress of the characters is unnaturally halted. The incomplete story denies easy satisfaction, thereby intentionally compelling the viewer to speculate. We assume at first that we are witnessing Aryan youth of the Third Reich, with the boy in front raising his right arm in a salute. However, a closer inspection of the background reveals quite the opposite: an urban North American street, and in the boy's hand is a table tennis paddle, lifted perhaps in order to ward off an oncoming ball. In contrast with another sequence taken—this one with girls on a bike—the typical pitched roofs and the subtitle "But National Socialist Germany..." leave no doubt as to its location. Why this misleading image of the young boys? Its placement between representations of Hitler uncannily contradicts the banality of the source material and eerily renders a pedestrian scene as horrific precisely because it is removed from a non-threateninq context and placed within a new context. How could life be so "normal" here while the horror was going on over there? Indeed, in a balanced construction Eisenberg opens his film with the boys whereas the penultimate sequence is that of the girls. Thus, through cinematic manipulation and editing, everyday life on Main St. USA is brought to Germany—displaced as it were—in the same way that Eisenberg connects with Hitler's visit to La Madeleine. Histories intersect, and in so doing questions are raised about larger networks of interconnectivity—whether given different circumstances such events might have been (and indeed were) possible elsewhere. Jacques Rancière, discussing Claude Lanzmann's *Shoah*, 1985, expresses fascination with the opening of the latter's film in which the present time is described. For Rancière,

It is through a confrontation between the words uttered here and now about what was and the reality that is materially present and absent in this place.... Today's scene resembles yesterday's extermination through the same silence, the same tranquility of the place, by the fact that today, while the film is being shot, as yesterday, when the killing machine was functioning, everyone is quite simply at their post, not speaking of what they are doing.[6]

By inserting a sequence from a non-European source, Eisenberg not only demonstrates how images wrested from their initial context can be used (and abused) willy nilly but also provocatively suggests that there may be more than a temporal link between the images.[7] But there is more, for although the clips are montaged anonymously some of the image quotations are familiar and resonate with a peculiar uncanniness precisely because they have been used before by another filmmaker, namely Ophüls. *The Sorrow and the Pity* is a compilation film, which draws heavily on documentary footage from the 1940s in order to understand European citizenry leading to the catastrophe of the Second World War. Ophüls, like Eisenberg is a *Displaced Person*—born in Vienna, he relocated with his parent to Paris during the 1930s. The events leading up to the Holocaust and the transformation of everyday life and people into perpetrators of crimes against humanity has been a recurring theme in Ophüls' oeuvre.[8] In *Displaced Person* quotes from Ophüls' masterpiece, thereby recycling the latter's images, and appropriating them into his own work. Such a strategy recalls the practice of cannibalism or androphagia (appropriated by Surrealists) in which the consumption and subsequent regurgitation of another was reserved only for those most worthy. Ophüls is evoked—a quote of a quote—the establishment of a cinematic historical continuum is produced based on a celluloid archive.

The spatial and geographical disturbance with which Eisenberg plays in *Displaced Person* finds its way temporally into *Cooperation of Parts*, 1987. Made six years later, *Cooperation of Parts*, as the title suggests, alludes to both the personal and professional arena of Eisenberg's life; the fragmentation he experienced as evidenced in his relationship to the Germany and Poland of his parents and the formal strategy of filmmaking by piecing together unexpected fragments. The film opens with footage taken by Eisenberg at a contemporary European train station (an amalgam consisting of exterior shots of the main train station in Calais and interior shots from the Gare de Lyon in Paris). However, the voice-over (Eisenberg's own) paradoxically—and reminiscent of Hollis Frampton's *Nostalgia* (*Hapax Legomena I*), 1971—announces:

Here is the oldest picture I've managed to obtain.... It's a picture of a young woman parting with friends at a railway station in Germany. There's no platform next to the train (the image on the screen negates this statement).... She's wearing dark sunglasses. Her hair is long and pinned in back.... We know that her two friends would finally arrive in the U.S. sometime in early 1949. So the photograph must be from the summer of 1948. She was trying to convince her own husband to emigrate to the U.S. as well.[9]

By juxtaposing images from 1983 France onto a verbal narrative that describes an unseen photo from a Germany of the late 1940s, Eisenberg relates the past to the present, and imbricates dialogue in a manner that recalls the Surrealist methodology of Walter Benjamin, in which the present and the past are interwoven through the complex interplay between the visual and audial registers. A similar consequence results from Eisenberg's treatment of the geographical France with Germany. Throughout the film this confusion of the senses prevails. Thus, Eisenberg continues is strategy of temporal and spatial crossing that originated in *Displaced Person*. Whereas in the former the intersections are only performed visually, in the latter they are further complicated. The effect produced is similar to that of a Vexierbild or picture puzzle—a representational trick made famous by Wittgenstein in his treatise on the Duck/Rabbit in which one image simultaneously reveals and hides another. In this instance, Eisenberg complicates the visual trope with sound—with eyes closed, Germany is evoked; with muted sound, France. The two exist together contrapuntally as one sound/image. This confusion of the senses is remarked upon in *Displaced Person* by Lévi-Strauss' voice-over when at one moment against a completely black screen he states, "could only exist by turning its back on the world of the senses; that is the world of the senses, the world we see, we smell, we taste, we perceive; that is a delusive world." Interestingly, Lévi-Strauss exempts hearing from his list of sense whereas, in fact, it is the only sense activated. Later, in *Cooperation of Parts*, an intertitle reads: "He's already begun to mistrust his sense, but not his senses." Of course, working with film the two primary senses that are utilized are seeing and hearing and their complex interplay is extremely significant. And although what we see is generally privileged due to its overpowering status as both evidence and witness, Eisenberg constantly underscores the importance of what we hear by forcing us to listen.

Returning to *Displaced Person* the sound track has no diegetic sound but is constructed of only two tracks: the performance of *Opus 59* and extracts from a 1977 radio lecture, "The Meeting of Myth and Science", broadcast in heavily accented English by the French anthropologist, Claude Lévi-Strauss.[10] The lecture came out of a series of interviews between Lévi-Strauss and Carole Orr Jerome and addresses the way in which man produces rational or scientific mythologies through which to understand and order the world. The two tracks play simultaneously and are carefully calibrated so that both remain decipherable and distinct at the same time. The two tracks serve different purposes, in terms of structuring devices as well as voice. The dual components of the track serve independent purposes evocative of contrapuntal composition in music. Contrapuntal composition, perfected by Bach in the eighteenth century, is based on the theory of two separate 'voices' that are brought together in one piece—very much like a musical rendition of a Vexierbild. Let us first examine Lévi-Strauss' speech. Acoustically it is framed by Beethoven's music and Lévi-Strauss distinctive voice begins a few minutes into the film after the introductory musical bars and visual frames. Despite the initial impression, the lecture has not been preserved in its entirety—although the order has been maintained. Eisenberg has cut several passages out of the original, but by suturing it together creates a harmonious flow. Where passages have been left out, the musical soundtrack is amplified, thereby filling the acoustic space with Beethoven's composition. The music between the spoken words corresponds approximately to the time it would take to read what Eisenberg has left out of the lecture. Thus the deletions are duly noted and not erased. As a visual correlative, Eisenberg has reprinted the written transcription of Lévi-Strauss' lecture leaving the struck through sentences and phrases in plain view. Thus, a trace or phantom voice remains. By truncating passages of the lecture, the meaning is altered and the significance of what Eisenberg has selected is increased. The lecture concerns the perceived gap between science and 'mythology' or to put it differently, the interplay of discourses of the irrational and the rational, order and disorder, understanding and confusion. In the lecture, Lévi-Strauss discusses the attempt to use science to clarify everything; instead, he proposes that there are some matters that simply cannot be explained by science. For instance, at one point he hypothesizes that, "there is (sic) a lot of things in life which can be reduced to physiochemical processes, which explain a part but not all", images of Hitler and his entourage of impassioned followers fills the screen. Against another sequences of images taken of Hitler viewing Notre Dame, Lévi-Strauss puzzles that "if the same absurdity was bound to reappear over and over again, and another kind of absurdity also to reappear, then there was something which was not absolutely absurd; or else it would not appear". By juxtaposing these words against the footage of Hitler, footage used repeatedly in *Displaced Person*, Eisenberg suggests that the phenomenon of Hitler was neither an isolated occurrence nor an anomaly but rather, a rational and calculable occurrence which could potentially and predictably recur.

In addition to Lévi-Strauss' meditations on how to explain certain phenomena, Eisenberg selects certain passages from the Lévi-Strauss lecture in which the latter comments on translation. Here Lévi-Strauss is explicit that translation is a process not just from one language into another but from one medium to another. He is adamant that meaning, significance, and understanding can be translated or transmitted to non-linguistic signifying systems, insisting that, "'to mean' means the ability of any kind of data to be translated in a different language. I do not mean a different language as French, German, or the like, but to be expressed, in different words, on a different level." Translation, similarly for Walter Benjamin, becomes less a system based on linguistic exactitude but more a *mode*.[11] Of key concern is whether one can translate across media into different codes. In the film, against the clip of formal dancers, Lévi-Strauss recalls his childhood drawings and muses about the possibility to try to express in one language, that is, the language of graphic arts and painting, something which also exists in music and which also exists in the libretto; that is, to reach the invariant property of a very complex let's not say code, but set of codes. There is the musical code, there is the literary code, and there is the artistic code and the problem is to find what is common to all of them. It's a problem, let's say of translation, to translate what is expressed in one language—or in one code, if you prefer... to be able to express it in a different language.

And of course, this is exactly what Eisenberg is attempting to assay—to see if it is possible to translate certain uncertainties and theoretical concerns into the audio-visual medium of an essay film.[12]

In addition to the significance of the meaning of the words, we also need to be attentive to the grain of the voice. In this instance, a translation process occurs in the traditional sense, that from French into English. But what is interesting is that in the English text spoken by Lévi-Strauss, his authorial presence is both maintained and respected. That his voice bears all the traces of the translation process, of the displacement of the French intellectual into a community of English speakers—the voice thus connotes a type of immigration or migration. More than conveying foreignness or otherness, a sense of time is also contained within the voice which bears the markers of age. It is not a young voice but one that belongs to a previous generation, one that has gone through the war. The voice then, is not merely a voice but because of its national origins and age, it is indeed a witness. Like documentary archival film stock, the voice bears the scars and traces of events, the first-hand knowledge of what happened, even though the immediate past is not mentioned directly in the lecture. However, because it is paired with images from that time period, it resonates, charged with surplus symbolic meaning. This is not to ignore the purely visual impact of the subjects caught by the camera, what Roland Barthes referred to as the "punctum" of the photographic image. These are moments which fleetingly pass by and create an impact but elude immediate connotative meaning (what Barthes terms "studium"). Here we can think of the zeal and fervor incorporated in the racing body and on the facial expression of the young woman chasing after Hitler on the train. Part of what makes *Displaced Person* such a complicated film is the excess of knowledge ("studium") that surrounds, contains and permeates the film. Both the spectator and Eisenberg know too much. Behind,

Displaced Person

within, and emanating out of every image of Hitler are the concentration camps and their victims. And this surplus of knowledge effects representation. As Rancière observes about witness narratives as a "new mode of art" that involves "not so much recounting the event as witnessing to a there was that exceeds thought, not only through its own particular surplus, but because the peculiarity of the there was in general is to exceed thought".[13] Within the tradition of documentary film this tendency towards material evidence is even more pronounced. The archival film stock comes both from a time past and as a recorder of that past. Made in 1981, *Displaced Person* was made before the digital revolution when a photographic or film negative was still believed to be real. Eisenberg's choice to use film stock as opposed to videotape is integral to his theory of image production as it relates to history and memory. All three films that comprise his German cycle, *Displaced Person*, *Cooperation of Parts*, and *Persistence* are made in film. He seeks the historical veracity of the material of celluloid that is not mediated by the introduction of a contemporary medium such as videotape. The found footage from non-fictional sources as well as from Ophüls' *The Sorrow and the Pity* all serve as witness and evidence. Further, the documentary genre points to the human hands and eyes behind the cinematic machine, the people who filmed the images. And in the case of Eisenberg this latter function is particularly significant when we realize that the footage from the train was taken by two camera teams—one on the platform and the other located just behind Hitler's shoulder. The formal staging and filming of history as an event meant to be recorded and transmitted is further underscored in an image towards the end of *Displaced Person* in which

Left and opposite:
Displaced Person

several military officers with cameras in their hands position themselves to get the perfect picture. Similarly, Eisenberg's films will enter into this cycle of history and contribute to these documents. The importance of using film in the 1980s and 1990s thus achieves even greater relevance for it also self-reflexively points to film's passing as a medium of documentation. For if the Second World War was witnessed in celluloid, today's wars are documented electronically. According to some film theorists such as David Rodowick, this shift to digital information radically transforms the representation of history. He argues, in both fiction and nonfiction cinema, the aesthetics and ethics of film are closely linked to historical powers of documenting and witnessing wherein the camera confronts the prior existence of things and people in time and in space, preserved in their common duration…. in the era of digital simulation, we are becoming resensitized to the powers of photography and cinema, especially since this experience is practically lost—it is already *historical*."[14]

To sum up thus far, the archival images and footage as well as the Lévi-Strauss lecture exist as fragments or as "shards [that] tell the story and prefigure the future." One element that stands outside of this structure, not only because it is whole, but also because it is outside the framed time period, is Beethoven's *Opus 59*, composed in 1808. How do we decode this music which transcends the other components? How does it function within the genre of non-fiction? What role does it play? In other words, the music goes beyond the empirical facts that have been assembled—it produces and locates an acoustical site within which the imaginary can

function. It thereby allows for that which is not grounded in the real—or science—but perhaps in the irrational—or myth—to enter.

Since the film is cued to the length of the composition, let us examine it as a basic structuring principle. We recall that within non-fiction film, the accompanying music goes back to the early moments of avant-garde cinema even before the advent of sound. We need only think of the artistic experiments by Fernand Legèr, Hans Richter, Viking Eggeling, Walter Ruttmann and others who sought to translate sonatas, opus, and symphonies into visual patterns of representation. The rhythmic dance of abstract forms across the screen or the carefully edited montage sequences were constructed to correspond to complex musical compositions. Certainly *Displaced Person* echoes *Opus 59* in the literal length of the piece, as well as the recurrent themes, motifs, and (sequence of) images that surface, similarly to certain instruments in the quartet announce their presence. Eisenberg explains, "It's not the usual phenomena in documentary, or in work that uses musical accompaniment, to have the music as the backbone, the structural backbone of the work. In *Displaced Person* many other events are hung on or woven through it... I was really trying to find a way to have people stay with it [the film], and the music sometimes allows that." Although Eisenberg stresses that the music functions primarily architecturally as a spine, I want to suggest that the central role of the music extends beyond the structure to include a thematic core as well.

In documentary, just as in feature fictional film, music is layered onto the soundtrack as a non-diegetic accompaniment. It is used to set the scene, produce emotional responses, punctuate certain actions and the like. Unlike the other sounds in non-fictional film which bear witness to the real, non-diegetic music, when used, pushes the documentary elements in the direction of fantasy. But in *Displaced Person* the use of music is far more complicated. Already in 1939 Brazilian-born filmmaker Alberto Cavalcanti observed that "Pictures speak to the intelligence. Noise seems to by-pass the intelligence and speak to something very deep and inborn... the picture lends itself to clear statement, while the sound lends itself to suggestion."[15] In other words, the visible world revealed to us in cinema is that of the rational, whereas the invisible but audible world corresponds to the irrational. Documentary images, rational objective images can be overturned, contradicted, and pushed into the space of imagination when coupled with radically different sounds. Instead of affirming what is visible, the music works contrapuntally to produce chance connections with often surprising effects that radically reframe vision. Claudia Gorbman has argued that non-diegetic music is not supposed to draw attention to itself. Rather its effects operate subconsciously on the spectator by subtly producing emotional states. However, sometimes music refuses to be silenced and in that case when "it calls attention to itself [it] swings away from the imaginary toward the symbolic".[16] And certainly by giving *Opus 59* such a central role in *Displaced Person* Eisenberg insists that we pay attention to the music.

In order to understand why *Opus 59* is preserved as a whole in *Displaced Person* in the otherwise visually war-shattered universe, it is necessary to look at the history of the piece. According to sound theorist, Michel Chion, unlike in the world of images, "music is something that carries no traces, that cannot be marked, and that has no scars. It remains untouched by history, by events, by horror."[17] Perhaps its essence does remain unaltered, but certainly the way it is heard changes. Musical historian,

Richard Leppert, argues that "hearing itself is historical; history determines a way of hearing. As a result, any of the myriad qualities immanent to a work either emerge or recede in relation to historical change."[18] How the quartet was heard in 1808 when it was first performed is different from how it may have been received in 1940 and subsequently how it is listened to in 1981 or 2010. As mentioned earlier, the quartets were commissioned by a Russian Count while Beethoven was in Vienna. The choice by Eisenberg of Beethoven is heavily loaded for it is well known that Beethoven was one of Hitler's three most beloved composers—the other two being Wagner and Bruckner. Still one may wonder why this particular composition was used. That Hitler spent a considerable amount of time working and studying in Vienna is not insignificant, and the Rasumovsky Quartets references his native city along with the historical and political connections between the former capital of the Hapsburg Empire and Paris. At the time of Beethoven's composition, Napoleon III was actively engaged in seeking to conquer Europe with Austria as the leading army in the coalition forces against French expansion. After Napoleon's defeat, a peace treaty was drawn up at the Congress of Vienna. Half a century later, Napoleon III lost the Franco-Prussian Wars after which Germany was united. Hitler's conquest of Paris thereby resonates with a larger historical trajectory that reverses the German loss to the French during the First World War and instead recalls the victorious nineteenth century. Eisenberg's choice of Beethoven recalls this history and the significance at the time of newsreel images recording Hitler's June 1940 visit.

However, Eisenberg evokes more than the French-German dynamic. Let us recall that the work was commissioned by Rasumovsky and that the musical qualities are supposed to have a certain "Russian" quality about them. Why does Eisenberg bring Russia into the Anglo-German-French constellation? The key lies in a photograph which he presents in *Cooperation of Parts*. Eisenberg's voice-over: "Here's another picture. It's of a music band, musicians and instruments." The photograph is

Eisenberg Family Photograph, 1944

of Eisenberg's father taken in 1944 in Kyrgyzstan in the Soviet labor camp. The handwritten note on the back of the photograph is misleading for it gives it a much later date in the hopes of obscuring the fact that his father was in a Russian labor camp and not a German one. Eisenberg's father, as a young communist in Warsaw before the war, like so many communists and socialists, fled to the East to escape the Germans, only to meet death or imprisonment by the Soviets.[19] His father always insisted "that it was his ability to make music that insured his survival." In the photograph, the instrument in Eisenberg's father's hands is an accordion. The other instruments in the photograph, with the exception of a set of drums, are string instruments: violins, mandolins and something resembling a banjo. The classical string quartet of Beethoven's *Opus 59* consists of two violins, a cello and a viola. In addition, to the quartet being based on contrapuntal composition—within ethnic symbolism, the violin is directly linked to the Jewish Diaspora and more recently to Auschwitz. I would argue then that Eisenberg wrests Beethoven's piece from Hitler and his audiences and instead forges a link to the Second World War, the fate of the Jews and more personally, as a gesture or recognition towards his father.

Beethoven becomes a cipher, and like La Madeleine, the meaning depends on the cultural and historical context in which the music is played. To that extent, Beethoven is a *Displaced Person* like the boys on the bicycle, or Hitler in Paris, or Lévi-Strauss' voice in his distinctive spoken English. The music morphs and changes like a chameleon or a virus depending on its context. Lawrence Kramer theorizes that "music adds something to other things by adding itself, but loses nothing when it takes itself away. By reason of this limitless subtractability, music has often formed the paradigm of autonomy not only in the modern system of the arts but also in the construction of subjectivity."[20] Beethoven's music draws us in and adds life to the otherwise mute images. Filmmaker Hartmut Bitomosky cautions that when sifting through archival footage it is important to bear in minds that "films may be the memory of their epoch,

Eisenberg Family
Photograph, 1944,
verso

but they are also what they have forgotten and what we cannot recall".[21] If the fragmentary nature of the image track breaks time and place, music does just the opposite, and keeps the spectator engaged with the images, it becomes the acoustic mortar in which the visual mosaic is set and which holds the whole together.

As mentioned, the archival footage is heavily manipulated by Eisenberg. It is repeated, slowed down, and further fractured, although such transformations of images still render them readable and distinguishable or recognizable. However, with music, although such manipulations are possible they must still be in motion or in play as it were. As the narrator of Jean-Luc Godard's *Allemagne 90 neuf zéro*, 1991, explains regarding the impossibility of narrating time, it would be "a bit like holding for an hour one single note, one chord, and trying to pass it off as music". Music, like time, must move forward in order to exist. There is no freeze frame for music, no still photography or still life. The etymology of cinema goes back to the Greek word for movement. It is a double movement not only within the frame but also of the frames of celluloid as they pass through both the camera and the projector. Since music has to move in order to exist, perhaps it is more closely an inherent and integral part of cinema than the images. The movement of the music, like that of history is inexorable; it cannot be frozen or stilled. Thus, *Displaced Person* self-reflexively comments on the cinematic machine and its relationship to history.

To conclude: *Displaced Person* is a film composed of recycled documentary images, and yet it is not a documentary—why not? This ambiguity is related to the soundtrack which produces associations and allows for free play and imagination. Thus, against the documentary images of the real, we hear music and thoughts. If we listen to the soundtrack another story emerges, a narrative which is sometimes contradictory, and at times parallel, or sometimes in synch with the images, but always it contains its own line of meaning. In this film, the images recall the absolute horror towards which instrumental reason led, and it is via the sound track that Eisenberg offers a possibility of hope. The assemblage of sounds and images in a non-codified, non-predictable manner allows for the production of a new aesthetic space.

Displaced Person provides a non-formulaic way of understanding the Holocaust. Both Beethoven and Lévi-Strauss counter the rational scientific machine of the Third Reich and allow the audience to listen to and hear alternatives. The words of Lévi-Strauss echo "there are a lot of things we have lost, and we should try, I'm not sure, to regain them, because I'm not sure that in the kind of world in which we are living and with the kind of scientific thinking we are bound to follow, we can regain these things exactly as if they had never been lost; but we can become aware of their existence and of their importance." *Displaced Person* forces both an awareness and a remembrance that is dictated not by history and scientific reason, but by the imagination.

~~THE MEETING OF~~

~~MYTH AND SCIENCE~~

~~CLAUDE LÉVI-STRAUSS~~

Now let me start with a personal confession. ~~There is a magazine which I read faithfully each month from the first line to the last, even though I don't understand exactly all of it: it is the Scientific American. I am extremely eager to be as informed as possible of everything that takes place in modern science and its new developments. My position in relation to science is thus not a negative one.~~ In the second place, I think there are a lot of things we have lost, and that we should try, I'm not sure, perhaps to regain them, because I am not sure that in the kind of world in which we are living and with the kind of scientific thinking we are bound to follow, we can regain these things exactly as if they had never been lost; but we can become aware of their existence and of their importance.

Now, in the third place, ~~my feeling is that modern science is not at all moving away from these lost things, but that more and more it is attempting to reintegrate them in the field of scientific explanation. The real gap, the real separation between science and what we might as well call mythical thought for the sake of finding a convenient name, although it is not exactly that the real separation occurred in the seventeenth and eighteenth century. At that time, with Bacon, Descartes, Newton, and the others, it was necessary for science to build itself up against the old generations of mythical and mystical thought, and it was thought that science~~ could only exist by turning its back upon the world of the senses, the world we see, we smell, we taste, we perceive; this was a delusive world, ~~whereas the real world was a world of mathematical properties which could only be grasped by the intellect~~ and ~~which was entirely at odds with the false testimony of the senses.~~

This was probably a necessary move, ~~for experience shows us that thanks to this separation—this schism if you like—scientific thought was able to constitute itself.~~

~~Now, my impression (and, of course, I do not talk as a scientist I am not a physicist, I am not a biologist, I am not a chemist) is that contemporary science is tending to overcome this gap, and that more and more the sense data are being reintegrated into scientific explanation as something which has a meaning, which has truth, and which can be explained.~~

~~Take, for instance, the world of smells. We were accustomed to think that this was entirely subjective, outside the world of science. Now the chemists are able to tell us that each smell or each taste has a certain chemical composition~~

~~and to give us the reasons why subjectively some smells or some tastes feel to us as having something in common and some others seem widely different.~~

~~Let's take another example. There was in philosophy from the time of the Greeks to the eighteenth and even the nineteenth century and there still is to some extent a tremendous discussion about the origin of mathematical ideas the idea of the line, the idea of the circle, the idea of the triangle. There were, in the main, two classical theories: one of the mind as a tabula rasa, with nothing in it in the beginning; everything comes to it from experience. It is from seeing a lot of round objects, none of which were perfectly round, that we are able nevertheless to abstract idea of the circle. The second classical theory goes back to Plato, who claimed that such ideas of the circle, of the triangle, of the line, are perfect, innate in the mind, and it is because they are given to the mind that we are able to project them, so to speak, on reality, although reality never offers us a perfect circle or a perfect triangle.~~

~~Now contemporary researchers on the neurophysiology of vision teach us that the nervous cells in the retina and the other apparatus behind the retina are specialized: some cells are sensitive only to straight direction, in the vertical sense, others in the horizontal, others in the oblique, some of them to the relationship between the background and the central figure, and the like. So and I simplify very much because it is too complicated for me to explain this in English this whole problem of experience versus mind seems to have a solution in the structure of the nervous system, not in the structure of the mind or in experience, but somewhere between mind and experience in the way our nervous system is built and in the way it mediates between mind and experience.~~

~~Probably there is something deep in my own mind, which makes it likely that I always was what is now being called a structuralist. My mother told me that, when I was about two years old and still unable to read, of course, I claimed that actually I was able to read. And when I was asked why, I said that when I looked at signboards on shops for instance, boulanger or boucher I was able to read something because what was obviously similar, from a graphic point of view, in the writing could not mean anything other than 'bou,' the same first syllable of boulanger and boucher. Probably there is nothing more than that in the structuralist approach; it is the quest for the invariant, or for the invariant elements among superficial differences.~~

~~Throughout my life, this search was probably a predominant interest of mine. When I was a child, for a while my main interest was geology. The problem in geology is also to try to understand what is invariant in the tremendous diversity of landscapes, that is, to be able to reduce a landscape to a finite number of geological layers and of geological operations.~~

Also I spent a great part of my leisure time as a child, as an adolescent boy, drawing costumes and sets for opera. The problem there is exactly the same—that is to try to express in one language, that is, the language of graphic arts and painting, something which also exists in music and which also exists in the libretto; that is, to reach the invariant property of a very complex, not say code, but set of codes. There is the musical code, there is the literary code, and there is the artistic code, and the problem is to find what is common to all of them. It's a problem, let's say, of translation—to translate what is expressed in one language—or one code, if you prefer, but language is sufficient—to be able to express it in a different language.

~~Structuralism, or whatever goes under that name, has been considered something completely new and at the time revolutionary; this I think, is doubly false. In the first place, even in the field of the humanities, it is not new at all; we can follow very well this trend of thought from the Renaissance to the nineteenth century and to the present time. But it is also wrong for another reason: what we call structuralism in the field of linguistics, or anthropology, or the like, is nothing other than a very pale and faint imitation of what the 'hard sciences,' as I think you call them in English, have been doing all the time.~~

~~Science has only two ways of proceeding: it is either reductionist or structuralist. It is reductionist when it is possible to find out that very complex phenomena on one level can be reduced to simpler phenomena on other levels. For instance,~~ there are a lot of things in life that can be reduced to physiochemical processes, which explain a part but not all. And when we are confronted with phenomena too complex to be reduced to phenomena of a lower order, then we can only approach them by looking to their relationships, that is, to try to understand what kind of original system they make up. And this is exactly what we have been trying to do ~~in linguistics, in anthropology,~~ and ~~in different fields.~~

~~It is true and let's personalize nature for the sake of the argument that Nature has only a limited number of procedures at her disposal and that the kinds of procedure which Nature uses at one level of reality are bound to reappear at different levels. The genetic code is a very good example; it is well known that, when the biologists and the geneticists had the problem of describing what they had discovered, they could do nothing better than borrow the language of linguistics and to speak of words, of phrase, of accent, of punctuation marks, and the like. I do not mean at all that it is the same thing, of course, it is not. But it is the same kind of problem arising at two different levels of reality.~~

It would be very far from my mind to try to reduce culture, ~~as we say in our anthropological jargon,~~ to nature, but nevertheless what we witness at the level of culture are phenomena of the same kind from a formal point of view (I do not mean at all substantially), but which raise at least the same problem to the mind that we can observe on the level of nature—of course, much more complex, much more complicated, and calling upon a much larger number of variables.

You see, I'm not trying to formulate a philosophy, nor even a theory. Since I was a child, I have been bothered by, let's call it the irrational, and trying to find an order behind what is given to us as a disorder.

~~It so happened that I became an anthropologist, as a matter of fact not because I was interested in anthropology, but because I was trying to get out of philosophy. It also so happened that in the French academic framework, where anthropology was at the time not taught as a discipline in its own right in the universities, it was possible for someone trained in philosophy and teaching philosophy to escape to anthropology. I escaped there, and was confronted immediately by one problem — there were lots of rules of marriage all over the world which looked absolutely meaningless, and it was all the more irritating because, if they were meaningless, then there should be different rules for each people, though nevertheless the number of rules could be more or less finite. So,~~ if the same absurdity was found to reappear over and over again, and another kind of absurdity also to reappear, then there was something which was not absolutely absurd; or else it would not reappear.

That was my first orientation, to try to find an order behind this apparent disorder. ~~And when after working on the kinship systems and marriage rules, I turned my attention , also by chance and not at all on purpose, toward mythology, the problem was exactly the same. Mythical stories are, or seem, arbitrary, meaningless, absurd, yet nevertheless they seem to reappear all over the world. A 'fanciful' creation of the mind in one place would be unique you would not find the same creation in a completely different place. My problem was trying to find out if there was some kind of order behind this apparent disorder that's all. And~~ I do not claim at all that there are conclusions to be drawn.

Now you raise the question of meaning without order… this I think, is absolutely impossible to conceive, ~~meaning without order. Their is something very curious in semantics, that the word 'meaning' is probably, in the whole language, the word the meaning of which is the most difficult to find.~~ What means 'to mean'? It seems to me that the only answer we can give is that 'to mean' means the ability of any kind of data to be translated into a different language. I do not mean a different language such as French, German, or the like, but to be expressed in other words on a different level. ~~After all, this translation is what a dictionary is expected to give you the meaning of the word in different words, which on a slightly different level are isomorphic to the word or expression you are trying to understand. Now, what would a translation be without rules? It would be absolutely impossible to understand. Because you cannot replace any word by any other word or any sentence by any other sentence, you have to have rules of translation. To speak of rules and to speak of meaning is to speak of the same thing, by Claude Lévi-Strauss~~ and if we look at all the intellectual undertaking of mankind, as far as they have been recorded and all over the world, the common denominator is always to introduce some kind of order. And if this is a basic need of the human mind and since, after all, the human mind is only part of the universe, well it's probably because there is some order in the universe ~~and the universe is not a chaos.~~

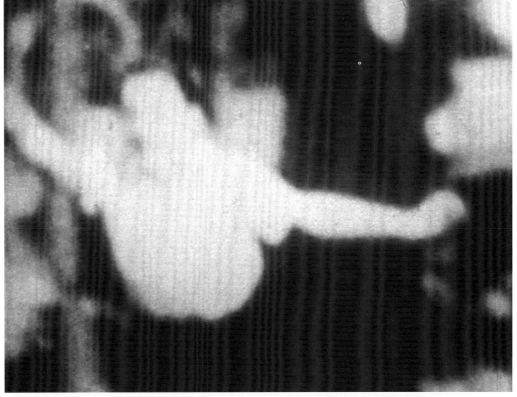

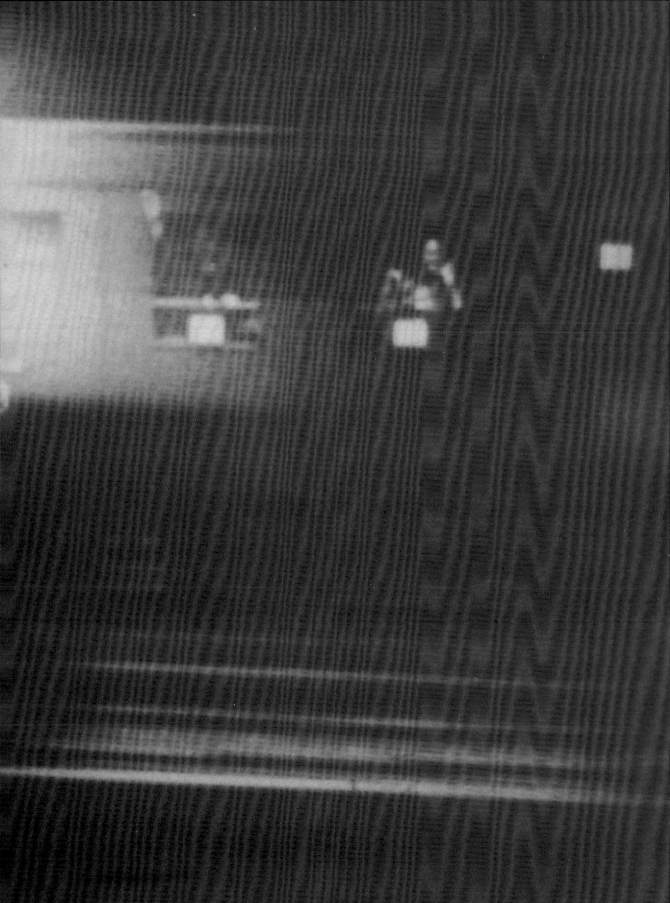

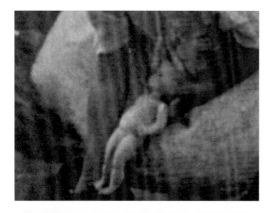

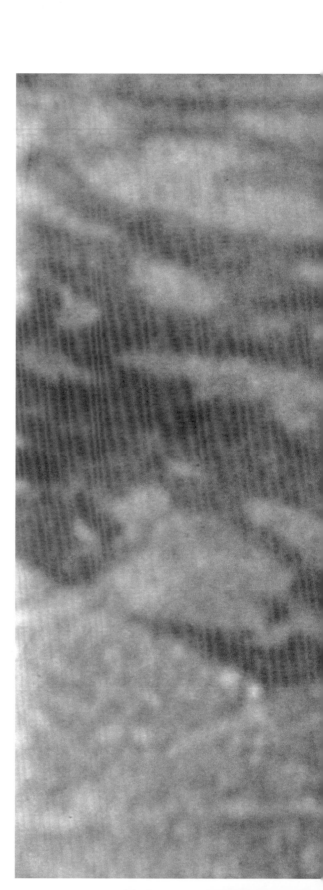

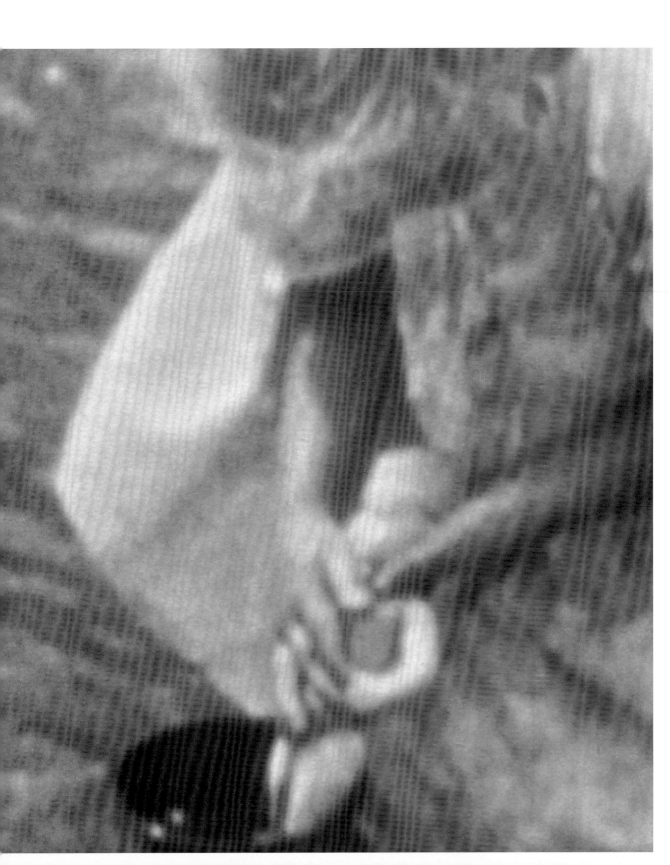

FRAGMENTS OF AN INHERITANCE
CONTINGENCES OF HISTORY IN *COOPERATION OF PARTS*

Jeffrey Skoller

The feeling is this: an anxiety... a phantom pain. Something unseen yet intensely present. How can I describe this feeling to you?
Text fragment from *Cooperation of Parts*

I.

Films end, but wars don't. Daniel Eisenberg, the son of survivors of the *Shoah*, returns, in his film *Cooperation of Parts*, 1987, to the scene of present-day Europe to explore relationships between his own present and his parent's past. This most overtly autobiographical of Eisenberg's films, engages traditions of autobiography and the diary film to explore relationships between personal identity and history showing how the force of a catastrophic history continues into the present despite the fact that the event itself ended long ago. In *Cooperation of Parts* there are no endings or beginnings; only fragments of image, sound and texts. These are bits and pieces of a trip, of events, moments, architecture, proverbs, thoughts. Eisenberg, born in Israel in the early 50s and raised in the United States, visits Northern Europe. Starting in France he travels to Berlin, then to Warsaw and Radom, Poland, the birthplaces of his mother and father, and to Auschwitz and Dachau where they were interred during the war.

Cooperation of Parts can be seen as part of a body of film, literature and other art works by the children of survivors of the *Shoah* that explore the ways in which their own lives have been structured by the past experiences of their parents. These works embody the trauma of the *Shoah* as it continues to reverberate across familial generations, both through fragmented narratives of the parents' experiences, but just as often in the lacunae of those narratives, the result of what cannot be spoken. In such works the process of their making becomes an occasion for the artists to confront those aspects of their personal histories which are largely unknown, but are nonetheless structuring of personality and world view. Such works of cinema, literature and art can be distinguished in temporal and qualitative ways from earlier works of Holocaust memory by survivors themselves (Levi, Wiesel, Appelfeld for example). In film, perhaps the most famous example is Alain Resnais' *Night and Fog*, 1955, which like *Cooperation of Parts* uses a voice-over essay form to attempt to think the meaning of the *Shoah*. Both films resist simple description of what occurred during the Nazi Holocaust and try to understand the problems of representing such an event as it recedes into the past. On the other hand, the temporal relationship of each film to the *Shoah* shapes each essay in distinctive ways. Jean Cayrol, himself a survivor of the Nazi camps, wrote the text of *Night and Fog* as an admonition to vigilance, that such a catastrophe might never happen again. As the first cinematic account of this history soon after the war, subjective and personal experiences of the events are carefully excised from the film, performing the assumption that catastrophes of such magnitude defy personal experience as a means of explanation. Eisenberg on the other hand, born after the event, can only explain the meaning of this history in terms of his own inherited relationship to it and the ways he has been formed by it. In *Cooperation of Parts* we see images Eisenberg filmed in the courtyard of his mother's apartment building from where she was deported to the camps.

Cooperation of Parts, Daniel Eisenberg, 1987

It was through her, not through her conscious intention that these things passed.

A voice over begins:

Like a shock wave felt through several generations. Its a typology, a magnetized personality. A personality characterized mainly by suspicion, mistrust, an uncanny ability to read the subtext. This personality is the one that draws negativity to itself. It's the one that people despise. The one that reverts to the defense of self; never a nation, never an idea. What happens if I discover who I am? What then?[1]

"Postmemory", is a term Marianne Hirsch has used to characterize "the experience of those who grow up dominated by narratives that preceded their birth, whose own belated stories are evacuated by the stories of the previous generation shaped by traumatic events that can be neither understood nor recreated."[2] Postmemory thus, is not simply the recollection of experience as much as it is introjected memory; memories that are at once one's own, but entirely mediated through projection and identification. Without concrete experience or even specific knowledge of the events, this next generation experiences their inherited past in the form of ephemeralities and hauntings that are sensed, intuited or gleaned from their highly attuned sensitivities to parents' moods and affects. It is this terrain, the most sophisticated of these works explore. The striking aspect of many of these works is the ways in which aesthetic form becomes a central concern for the artists creating them. In highly varied ways, each must devise new ways to articulate their own place in these histories. Such films vary in aesthetic approach from highly experimental hybrid forms that mix documentary, animation and abstract imagery in Abraham Ravett's films *Everything's for You*, 1989 and *The March*, 1999, to observational and allegorical forms in Chantal Ackerman's *D'est*, or the interview/testimonial documentary form, as in Jack Fisher's *A Generation Apart*, 1984. Other experiments in narrative form can be seen in such para-cinematic works as Art Spiegelman's famous graphic docu-novel *Maus* and the illustrated memoir *I Was the Child of Holocaust Survivors* by Bernice Eisenstein, 2006.

In all of these examples, the artists find it necessary to invent innovative and often unique forms that can adequately address the ephemerality, gaps and limits of what can be represented and understood about the lives, not just of their survivor/parents, but more crucially their own. The process of representing the often fragmented and repressed knowledge defies conventional narrative forms that are structured to create illusions of

The March, Abraham Ravett, 1999

clarity and completeness. For these artists, their very subject position has created the necessity for new ways of using their medium that can allow for what cannot be known or explained through conventional storytelling or even language. Such forms emphasize questions rather than exposition, process over closure, affects rather than analysis. Instead of creating works that separate past from present by constructing a gap between then and now, these works focus on the present as the point where the past is created. What is understood of the past is mediated through an active engagement with the conditions of the present rather than singular recollections of past experience.

In many of these works, this distinctive relation to time emerges in the direct confrontation between parents and their now adult children, who are demanding that parents engage with their need to know these histories. In the films of Ravett and Fisher for example, we see how the process of filming itself becomes a context for the son's on-camera exhortation of his parents to try to speak the missing fragments of their stories. Thus in *The March*, Ravett filmed his mother every year for 13 years, each time asking her to tell him what happened on the "death march" out of Auschwitz that she miraculously survived. Similarly in Spiegelman's graphic docu-novel we see him showing up at his recalcitrant father's house with a tape recorder insisting he tell his story. Such works focus on the relationship between parent and child in the present as the artists attempt to transform the stuttering inconsistencies of memory to representation. At the same time, they are engaging ethical questions of, on the one hand, the responsibility of the parent/survivors to impart their experiences—the traumas of which the children have inherited—and on the other, they reveal the often aggressive ways the children exhort their often fragile parents, to recall and explain their experiences.

In *Cooperation of Parts*, Eisenberg similarly uses the process of making the film to explore the fragments of his historical inheritance. But rather than the kind of direct confrontation with his parents we see in Ravett and Spiegelman, Eisenberg extricates himself from the familial circle to explore this fragmented legacy on his own. His parents unable to supply the knowledge he seeks, Eisenberg journeys out into the world from where they came—alone. Returning to Europe, the scene of that history, his concerns move beyond his parent's personal experiences of the *Shoah* to question his own existence in relation to Europe itself. In this sense *Cooperation of Parts* is the pilgrimage of a young American back to the place his parents were born, the seat of the culture which both formed him and which mobilized its immense power and knowledge to eradicate his family.

D'Est, Chantal
Akerman, 1993

II.

In *The Arrival of a Train at La Ciotat Station*, Lumiere Brothers, 1895, a film that marks the beginning of cinema and imminently of the twentieth century, we see a train pulling into the station and coming to a stop. Utopian in its vision, like all arrivals it is a hopeful moment: people disembark from the train, greet one another. There is a sense of possibility. Newness seems to abound in this short strip of film, as one experiences the excitement of the new technologies of transportation and the new imaging device that create this moment. The motion picture camera and motorized transportation are both central to the development of the twentieth century. Now nearly a century later, the film *Cooperation of Parts*, starts with the train leaving the station and begins a journey of the uncanny, at once an exploration of foreign lands and a homecoming. The camera is now on board the train—camera and train have become one, gliding over the well-used rails of twentieth century Europe. This time the view is decidedly dystopic; the close-ups of the rails and blurred trees, photographed from inside the car, raise the specter of a century of deportations, emigrations and dislocations. The image of the railroad no longer signifies the possibility of beginnings, the opening up of new sights, and ways of living as it did at the turn of the century; it now contains the ominous quality of endings and severings.

On board and returning to the site of his parent's early life, Eisenberg questions his own identity in relation to this place, which in counter-life might have been his own world. His parents' miraculous survival of the extermination camps, their post-war meeting, marriage and the creation of a family—Eisenberg's very existence—all are contingent to the Nazi narrative of Jewish genocide. This child was never supposed to be born, and this film never made. As Mark McElhatten writes: "Eisenberg marvels at the very fact that he exists at all. Seeing himself as a statistical oddity in light of the numbers exterminated and the numbers that survived, "by all rights or reason I should not exist."[3]

The problem of how to construct an identity in the context of a European culture that he is inextricably a part of, but which also tried to annihilate his family and people permeates his experience. It is central to this film. It is the sense of being in between, at once inside and outside.

So I wind up asking the same question my mother asks, Why me?[4]

Left: *Arrival of a Train at La Ciotat*, August and Louis Lumière, 1895

Right and opposite: *Cooperation of Parts*

This is Eisenberg's burden. Having been born into catastrophe that was not his own, like being exposed to radioactive material, his parents' catastrophe becomes his, and he has little choice in the matter and even less context. He is forced to live in the shadow of events and experiences that not only were never his, but are never rendered clearly for him, spoken of only in hushed tones and disconnected stories. Alone, he is left to sift through the fragments of past events that are never fully explained or articulated.

It is in this uneasiness that the war beyond its end continues nevertheless, which Eisenberg explores through image and sound fragments. As he states:

The fragment contains within it an implied reference to something that was once whole. It suggests damage and violence, time and distance. These qualities I found were integral to my own constitution and it was with the making of *Cooperation of Parts* that this became clear.[5]

The filmmaker returns with his camera to the scene as both a ghost and a living embodiment of history. The images of the graves, crematoria, the stable-like bunk houses, guard towers and barbed wire are now well known from the stream of films over the years. Resnais' *Night and Fog* once again comes to mind. With its gliding elegiac tracking shots through the rooms and fields of Auschwitz, *Night and Fog* showed for the first time post-war images of the camps. Quintessentially modernist, the long smooth tracking shots hovering above human eye level were meant to be revelatory, rendering visible that which is hidden and unseeable both of the past and the present. The objective movements of the seamless lateral pans revivifying the now dormant death camp becomes a morality tale—an admonition—for what must be seen as the mind-boggling evidence of what occurred in this place accumulates at the edges of the frame. The forward moving camera in *Night and Fog* is redemptive, holding within it the promise that with a continuing awareness of what occurred through what can be seen, it will make it harder for what happened to happen again.

While the scenes are familiar, the camera work in *Cooperation of Parts* is very different. 35 years later, the camera is now hand-held, at eye level, attached to the filmmaker's body. Eisenberg is not only recording what is in front of the lens, but also his body's movements—foot-steps, arm and hand movements—a subjective record of what catches Eisenberg's attention. While the camera mounted on tracks in *Night and Fog* is expository, the jagged searching hand-held camera of *Cooperation of Parts* is exploratory, probing, incredulous. What can actually be known of this place?

Eisenberg uses the motion picture camera as a kind of conjuring tool to invoke that history, as if it lay dormant in the ground, the architecture, the fence posts and guard towers of the death camps, the railroad tracks. We see ephemeral reflections of people in windows looking out—but at what? We see the edge of the mass graves, statues and frescos in buildings pockmarked by bullets. The camera is never able to fix on a single image, as if the ground is solid one moment and then liquefied the next. What we see are image shards, off-kilter compositions, wisps of light. Is the filmmaker's eye searching for evidence, for meaning? But what is there to be seen? At Auschwitz, the camera pans over the camp's grounds, moves obsessively through the empty bunk rooms. It peers into the now clean crematoria ovens, examines artifacts left by the prisoners; it inspects in close-up the dirt roads and pathways of the camp. Is he looking for some proof of or key to his parents' experiences through some kind of elision of past and present, or more information about what occurred there and why? But the images are dumb, they reveal little except for what can be seen on surfaces or of crumbling remaining objects. Photographing the site at which so many were lost and countless others' lives were shaped and reshaped—his own included—the place reveals nothing of who they were or why they were destroyed. For a postmodern filmmaker like Eisenberg, the camera is used to reveal the limits of what can be seen and known. That an image of a place could reveal the secrets of an event by gazing upon it or that his subjectivity could clarify the silent history of a landscape is impossible.

Just as these scenes evoke, but don't reiterate the modernism of *Night and Fog*, so too does Eisenberg's distinctive use of the hand-held, subjective camera evoke the lyrical modernism of the first-person cinema of the American avant-garde, as his camera gives a direct image of the filmmaker's subjective perceptions and embodied responses. There is a surface affinity to the subjective camera work of the avant-garde filmmakers, such as Stan Brakhage, Bruce Baillie and others. However, in these films such first person camera work was understood as a vision of revelation rendering visible the most subjective impulses of the filmmaker.[6] Eisenberg's use

Production still of *Night and Fog*, Auschwitz, setting up tracks for camera dolly
Source: BFI

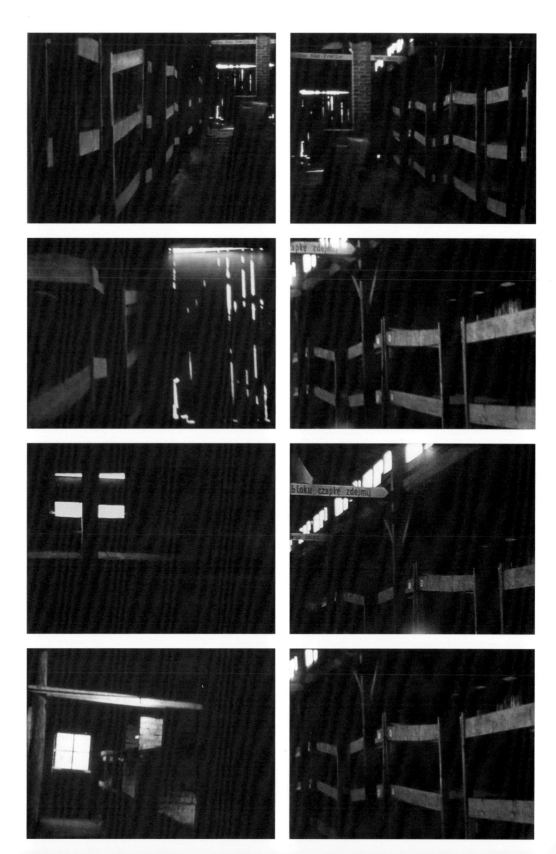

of the hand-held camera has a different agenda. He is not so much interested in personal revelation as in the revelation of the limits of the specular and empirical.

The shaky, often blurred images that rarely form a fixed composition emphasize the surface nature of film images—shape, color, light. The flat beauty of the images insist that there is no underneath—little to be uncovered or revealed. The images are what they are.

In *Cooperation of Parts*, Eisenberg and his camera stand as witness to what can never be completely known or understood. At Auschwitz what he finds are questions and more questions. At times Eisenberg tries to give the image primacy over language, but there are few answers. His camera can record an index of what he points it at. It can register his movements, but there is only the blunt image of the present.

This inability of his images and the specular itself to render visible a hidden legacy leads Eisenberg back to language. As the camera fitfully explores the grounds of camps, graveyards, monuments, city streets and the facades of buildings, the voiceover always returns. The voice, constantly probing, is in turn confused, speculative, judgmental, philosophically self aware, even child-like:

I have the illusion that nothing of great importance will be revealed. It's a place of disasters, of the failure of will. Everything reminds me of you... I asked simple questions, responses were measured. What were they looking at? Why couldn't they go? How was it that you were there?[7]

At these moments of incommensurability between the images and Eisenberg's questions, the filmmaker returns to language for grounding. Interspersed throughout the film, we see and hear short proverbs and aphorisms, some taken from Yiddish lore, some from contemporary thinkers, some remembered from childhood. They too are fragments, at times synecdochical, and appear throughout this work both as spoken and written text. These proverbs can be analytical tools, jump starting the viewer into thought. Often they appear together as text and speech, over black, no image to be seen. At other times they are rhythmic incantations of oblique evocations of his parents' lives over images of cityscapes and the landscape of the camps. In one sequence Eisenberg's camera explores the ruins of an old Jewish graveyard, as he describes a photograph (presumably) of his father as a member of a musical band while in a Soviet Labor camp. The voice-over speculates that it was his ability to play music that saved his life.

But more often, in the context of the history Eisenberg is searching for, the aphorisms seem ironic and damning of the culture that produced them, as in a sequence where we see the foundation stones of the prisoners' barracks, marking off the absent buildings at Dachau with an aphorism about 'The one road to Freedom' which admonishes 'obedience', 'diligence', 'honesty', 'cleanliness', 'sacrifice' and 'love of one's country.' The jagged relationship between image and text, hearing and seeing, listening and reading, further emphasizes the fragmentary nature of this history, and as well the limits of both language and image to represent the totality of the filmmaker's experience. This is ultimately what separates this work from the modernist tradition of the lyrical personal film.

Cooperation of Parts is a son's journey to war, a war into which he was born. He is a part of a series of events that were as random and unpredictable as who survived the war and who didn't. In its final scenes we are in the courtyard of the apartment where his mother once lived in Radom, Poland. The courtyard is now filled with blonde-haired children playing, skipping rope, playing cat's cradle. Clothes hang on the line; the mortar is crumbling from the walls of the building. The camera watches the children closely: their feet, elbows, how they touch each other. Again only fragments— the camera moves on ground that is not solid. Where are we located in time? Is this moment the past? the present? a memory? a dream? a wish? And whose moment is it? The final shot is a subjective camera moving down a Radom Street; the compositions are again fragmented, off-centered. The final titles appear:

Going down that street ten thousand times in a lifetime...
or perhaps never at all....[8]

"Or perhaps..." This final phrase of the film, with all of its sense of possibility and the randomness of chance, is the central motif of this film. Eisenberg's journey and the very film we are watching can be seen to cast a sideshadow (the illumination

Cooperation
of Parts

of the multiple contingencies that surround the outcome of an event) on the *Shoah*, which interrupts the narratives of inexorability of total annihilation that surrounds Jewish history.[9] At the same time the film sideshadows his own life, contemplating it as a series of contingencies. Could he have just as easily grown up in his mother's courtyard in Poland, as in the United States or never even have existed at all? *Cooperation of Parts*, explores the way historical events can never be contained by the singular line of inevitability, but rather, how events are inflected by chance and the personal and political choices that are constantly being made. The importance placed on this notion of contingency in history in the film is exemplified in its fragmented and open form.

The film works to liberate the history of the *Shoah* from the dehumanizing effects of singular and inexorable history. Placing the imaginings of what might have or what could have happened alongside of the reality of what did, doesn't lessen the power of the horror of what happened to the people who once lived in this apartment building 40 years earlier. But having the what-might-have-been co-exist with the what-did-happen releases the victims from a helpless sense of their history as destiny to be passively lived with and begins to untangle the idea of fate from history. It asserts that history is actively worked on and worked through—not simply given.

Left and opposite:
Cooperation of Parts

going down that street
ten thousand times in a lifetime.....

III.

Part of what makes a work like *Cooperation of Parts* so valuable as a radical example of new possibilities for narrating such difficult themes is the way it unbinds the events referenced throughout the film from a formulaic narrative of redemption in which the filmmaker's existence, as the child of Holocaust survivors, can be understood to provide closure to the horror of that event. In this film, there is no linear trajectory that moves to resolution as do more conventional cinematic "Holocaust histories" such as *Schindler's List*, Steven Spielberg, 1993. In that paradigmatic film, like *The Wizard of Oz* in negative, we are brought from the black and white "filmstocked" nightmare of the carnage of northern Europe into the bright color daylight, to the final redemption of Eretz Israel, where we find the remnants of the real "Schindler Jews" being lead to a grave by the actors who played them in the drama. Together they place stones on the real Schindler's grave. Schindler has died, his Jews survived, we have survived. The film ends. The Holocaust ends, they have become one and the same. By contrast, in *Cooperation of Parts*, there are no cathartic moments of revelation or transformation to give closure to the narrative. Though the film recounts personal experience, and at times is even autobiographical, Eisenberg is never content to simply become the traumatized subject that is at the center of a drama of victimhood. He never uses the work as a confessional to give authority to his experience—as if the testimony of personal experience was somehow more authentic and less mediated or stylized than any other narrative form. Nor does this work function as a kind of therapeutic device for the self-healing of the artist's personal wounds. Eisenberg is

first and foremost, a creative artist who is exploring and thinking through multiple positions in the world he was born into.[10]

But this is not life we are experiencing. It is a film, a highly stylized and rigorously constructed work of art which also raises questions about the nature of making meaning through cinema. Throughout the film, one can see the process of the filmmaker trying to construct workable narratives for representing his experience, his parents' experience, a European Jewish experience. But he doesn't stop there. This is too simple; it leaves out too many complexities and contradictions. Rather than creating the illusion of coherence by employing devices that produce a rational linear narrative leading to specific conclusions, Eisenberg creates multiple pasts and presents through layers of fragmented images, sounds, voices and scenarios. The relationship between meanings generated and the truth of those meanings is constantly being placed in question. Filmmaker Trinh T. Minh-Ha has referred to the space between truth and meaning as the "interval":

Truth and meaning: the two are likely to be equated with one another. Yet what is put forth as truth is often nothing more than a meaning. And what persists between the meaning of something and its truth is the interval, a break without which meaning would be fixed and truth congealed.[11]

Finally, although *Cooperation of Parts* has elements of both the historical documentary and the lyrical autobiographical film, it is first and foremost a work of art. It is an experience that sensitizes the viewer to the possibilities of the past by producing a history which allows for an engagement with randomness, contradiction and contingency. The work is permeable; there are spaces for multiple readings, interpretations, even incomprehension. The viewer is able to think through what is seen and heard in the text and relate that to what s/he knows or has experienced.

Perhaps most importantly, in *Cooperation of Parts*, time is not simply a representational element, pretending to move into the past via theatrical means as in the conventional historical drama. The viewer is not projected into the screen as if it were a time capsule and taken into a new time zone. Here time is a material element, the duration spent with an image, time spent thinking and listening. These are physical and phenomenological processes. The film uses its duration to generate its own present/its presence—and ours. Time creates a space between the screen/film and viewer—a place for thought. This space between—also an interval—allows the viewer to experience herself in relation to the images and words, and even (or especially) to experience the silences and ruptures of meaning. It is in this space between image and viewer where it becomes possible to grapple with loss, the implications of what a Holocaust might mean and with the limits of how that can possibly be understood. Unlike *Schindler's List*, which is structured around themes of transformation and redemption, neither occurs at the end of *Cooperation of Parts*. Eisenberg doesn't find his 'true' identity, nor does he come to understand his parent's experience better, nor does he put it all behind him. What one is left with is the document of an attempt.

Perhaps this work can be seen most purely as an essay film—neither pure history, philosophy, nor autobiography. Eisenberg attempts to engage with past events, with the possibility of constructing an identity in relation to the overwhelming contingencies that structure his existence. Throughout the film, he is at once representing this process and resisting its representation. In the fragmentation that occurs through this contradiction, one begins to understand the complexity of his position, and like Eisenberg himself, one begins to ask questions.

Cooperation of Parts suggests a different kind of formal and conceptual possibility for using cinema to interrogate a complex, multi-dimensional catastrophe of the proportions of the *Shoah*. In so doing, it suggests an ethics for representing the past that breaks with conventional linear, causal narrative forms. 65 years after the Second World War, if learning about the *Shoah* is to become an integral part of education in today's society, then we also need an ethics of representation for that event. Such an ethics would include a way of producing art from catastrophe that does not dehumanize the living victims, the memory of the dead, and the viewers. As I have argued here, *Cooperation of Parts* is a model for such an ethics. Like the most radically ethical contemporary art it challenges the modernist aura of essential meanings, calling into question narratives that are linear, universalized or triumphalist versions of history on the one hand or are hierarchies of horror and suffering on the other. This is the challenge of a 'postwar' aesthetics: to honor the specificity of past events and histories that occurred, while at the same time, to continue to invent new forms which allow such histories to reverberate and inflect the present with possibility.

Cooperation of Parts

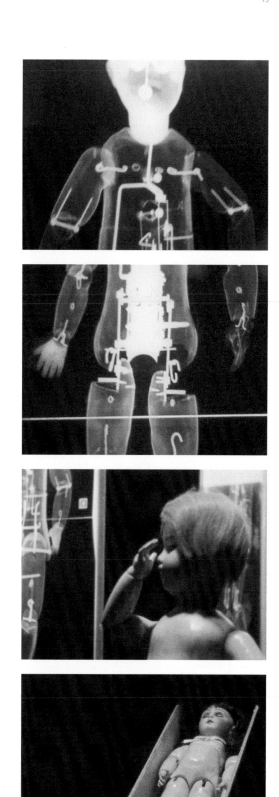

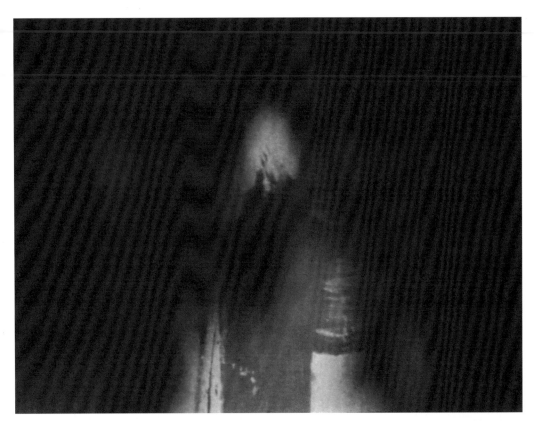

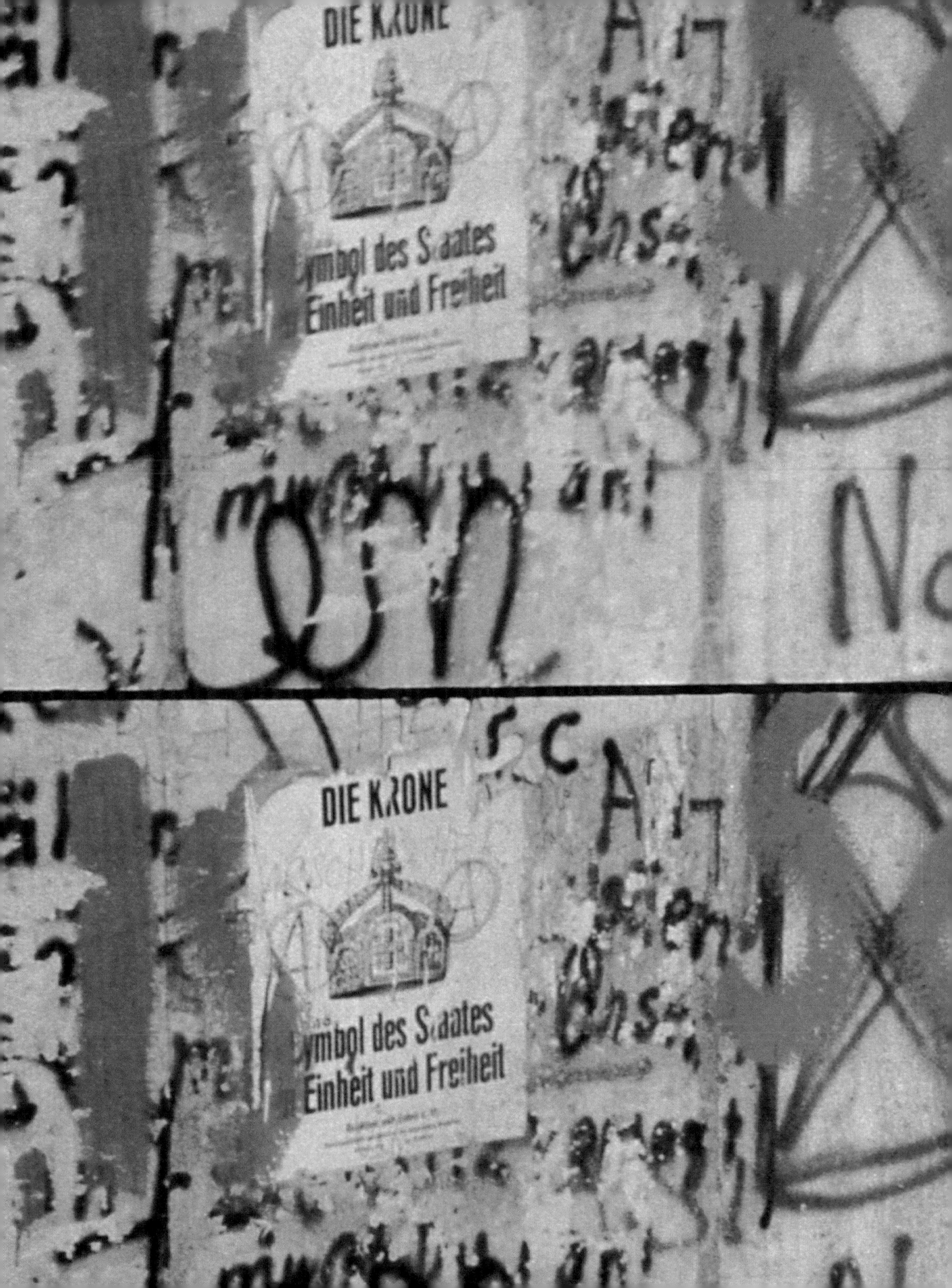
DIE KRONE
Einheit und Freiheit

LOOKING ACROSS THE THRESHOLD

PERSISTENCE AS EXPERIMENT IN TIME, SPACE, AND GENRE

Leora Auslander

Using footage both old and new, music, sound effects, text, and the spoken word, Daniel Eisenberg's *Persistence* Film in *24 absences/presences/prospects*, 1997, offers its audience a reflection on time, memory, history, and repetition, in Germany from 1933 to 1992. The film is divided into 24 "scenes", which move through time but far from linearly. Eisenberg takes our eyes across images as visually unlike as the wreckage of Braunschweig and Berlin at the conclusion of the Second World War to the beautiful, regular, reassuring alleys of the formal gardens at the Schloss Charlottenburg and on to the uncanny, museumified spaces of the former headquarters of the East German secret police or of the rooms used for human experimentation at the concentration camp at Sachsenhausen. Many images are echoed in others, most often from another time. The devastation of the Second World War reappears, in much milder form, in the bleakness of the minimally-renovated cityscapes the G.D.R. left behind. The never-seen American warplanes from which much of the archival footage Eisenberg uses are evoked in the rusting remnants of the Soviet Airforce in Berlin of the early 1990s. Remnants of 'hot' war are thus reprised in those of the Cold. The Siegessäule, Berlin's iconic winged statue of Victoria, that can be read as angel, also comes and goes in the film, bringing with it Walter Benjamin's vision of history. Those images are punctuated visually by titles and texts that sometimes provide orientation and sometimes demand reflection and aurally by both music and occasionally by a British radio voice providing the time. Voiceovers provide another counterpoint. The distinctively American voice reads a variety of often beautiful and always carefully crafted prose, which always resonates with both the written text and visual images but not necessarily in immediately apparent ways. Often, while the viewers' eyes are in one time and space, Eisenberg takes our ears to another, jostling our expectations of synchronicity. Finally, the film is lightly peopled; it is the built environment and nature that take center stage. *Persistence* is a history of destruction and starting over, brutality and humaneness, despair and hope. The history of Berlin, in other words, from 1933 to 1992.

What happens when a historian, as a historian and not in one of the other selves she also inhabits, confronts Daniel Eisenberg's *Persistence*? In my case, a rather dizzying combination of fascination, admiration, and disorientation. Those emotions are generated by the subject, the medium, and the genre of the work. How the past continues to be part of the present; the radical ruptures that characterized German history in the twentieth century; the rhetoric of history telling; the relation of big politics and the minutiae of everyday life; and, the annihilation of Germany's Jews and attempted reconstruction of that community are all central to both the film and not only to my work, but that of many others who earn their living writing history. *Persistence* thus feels very familiar, very insightful, very moving and very important, but also very challenging. That challenge came from the fact that while the issues raised in *Persistence* are familiar to a historian of modern Europe, its genre is not. It is a film, not a book or an article, and it is not a documentary film. It is, furthermore, simultaneously and vividly an analysis of historical processes and a document of its time. It has, in other words, an interpretation of post-war and post-unification German society at the same time as it could be used by historians as a source to better understand Germany of the early 1990s. *Persistence* forces reflection on what historians expect to encounter in both historical analysis and the traces past moments or epochs leave behind that provide the basis for future scholarship.

Historians generally assume that work contributing to advancements in our knowledge of the past, as opposed to those that serve to diffuse such knowledge to a broader public, follow a set of explicit and implicit ground rules.[1] The exposition takes narrative form, in prose, and on paper. That narration is based on research primarily in libraries and archives with written sources, although oral histories, music, maps, photographs, films, music and material culture are increasingly accepted as legitimate forms of (supplementary) evidence. The empirical basis for the story told is documented through footnotes which specify, in so far as possible, the authorship, date and place of production, genre, and current location of each source used. The scholarly apparatus is designed to enable other scholars to both verify the sources and the interpretations of those sources and to build on the research. And, while most historians have long acknowledged the limited truth claims we can make, the goal remains, nonetheless, to write the 'true story'.[2] Finally, historians expect their readers to bring their rational, rather than emotional or aesthetic, faculties to bear when assessing their work. It is accepted that other genres of the telling of the past, on paper, in museums, on stage or television and in the cinema, will not follow these rules, but, and this is crucial, historians don't expect to learn anything from these forms of presenting a historical narrative. These are sites of popularization, not where understanding is deepened and interpretations modified.[3]

Persistence, a film that refuses the narrative conventions of the documentary and one that furthermore is not a popularization or presentation of historians' research on post-war Germany but rather its own intervention, radically disrupts this schema. That intervention lies not with providing viewers with information about that history, nor with an explanation, nor a narrative line. Rather, *Persistence* confronts its audience with a challenging vision of how the past works in the present, radically unsettling our conceptions of time, and history itself, in the process.

As a film, and as a film that refuses many of the narrative conventions of film-making, it can do many things that academic history texts cannot. First, and most obviously, it interpolates its audience not just as viewers, but equally crucially, as listeners and readers. *Persistence* takes the viewers' eyes across contemporary and archival footage as well visual citations from Roberto Rossellini's *Germany, Year Zero*, 1948, at the same time as our ears are taking in a complex melding of texts, sound effects, and music. Some of the aural words reappear, or appear initially, as text on the screen. There are, of course, no footnotes; most of the documentation for all the forms of citation—visual, musical, and textual—is provided only at the end of the film, although some of the texts provide sources. The concluding credits are, furthermore, not keyed to specific moments in the film so if one does not recognize the citation it's difficult to be sure of the sources. Some clearly influential sources—like Walter Benjamin's work—are not named at all. It is a version of telling the past that involves the ears as much as the eyes, affect as much as rationality, and works aesthetically as much as argumentatively. The film itself, as much as what it depicts, is, in other words, an object to be reckoned with. It is far from transparent and certainly does not merely document or represent. In its self-assertion, it poses particular challenges to an academic historian whose profession teaches effacement of the prose we write in favor of the story told. Historians strive to write clearly, lucidly, even elegantly, but beautiful historical prose is prose that mostly isn't noticed, that doesn't get in the way of the story. The physical objects carrying the words—books—too, are to be as unobtrusive as possible, merely porters of words.

Finally, not only is *Persistence* a film about history, but, the shooting having concluded in 1992 and the film itself finished in 1997, it is now a historical artifact that may be read as a source, yielding information about that post-unification moment. While this is of course true of all works of historical analysis—a book of academic history researched in the early 1990s and published in 1997 too has become an artifact of that moment—the nature of *Persistence* makes it even truer. Eisenberg self-consciously situates his film, and his interpretation, in the moment of its production. In their quest for objectivity and for respect for the integrity of the past, most historians strive to efface the present, to write as if the only influence of the time in which they live lies in the conversations in which they engage with other historians. Even though most professional historians acknowledge that we write out of and for the present, writing responsibly, as a historian, does not usually entail discussion of either how the historian's individual present or the major events of the day shape the history written. Such reflexivity is, in fact, generally viewed with suspicion, the author thought to be indulging in narcissism or to be guilty of presentism. Except for historians of later generations seeking to write the history of their discipline, therefore, such histories are only marginally useful as sources yielding information on their era to be mined by later historians. *Persistence*, by contrast, forces the viewer to admit that both she and the film's maker are historically located and will, in our turn, become part of the past. Given that almost 20 years have passed since the movie was filmed and 13 years have now elapsed since the film's production, the historian's source antennae quiver at the readings of post-unification Germany that this film allows.

This is, in sum, a film that provokes historians, or at least this one, to unexpected ruminations on how to think about these theoretical and historical questions. My own long dissatisfaction with the way boundaries are drawn between present and past, and the rhetoric of historical exposition of my discipline, has made the provocation particularly welcome. This essay has therefore become a series of ruminations/meditations in written word and still images solicited by the melding of Daniel Eisenberg's own filmed images, archival footage, written and spoken words, sound effects and music in the episodes of his film, *Persistence*.

PRESENCE/STANDPOINT I

Very early in the film, the first scene in fact after the title, after being given a moment to absorb in silence the extraordinarily beautiful, eerily unpeopled although very much alive with wildly growing greenery, ruin of the Elisabethskirche, we are told by the voiceover that it is May 1983. The fact that the church is in East Berlin is signaled by the voice telling us that it has arrived at this spot having traversed the border and submitted to customs and dealt with the currency exchange. After a few minutes, we catch a glimpse of two young men moving about the church with surveying equipment. At the same time the distinctively American voice, that one assumes to be the filmmaker's, resumes, recounting in the first person his disappointment with the fact that passers-by on the street were completely unnoticing of this magnificent ruin. He waited for a reaction, there was none, and he left. This strikes the viewer/listener oddly, since he seems to still be there and, if no one was paying attention, then what are the surveyors doing there? The confusion is unresolved as film carries us seamlessly eight years forward (into the post-unification period) when East Berlin has become simply Berlin. Much appears to be static. The ruins are lit by an unchanging sun, nature continues to reassert itself challenging the human-made masonry. (It seems, in fact, all to have been filmed at one time.) But much has changed. Instead of meeting indifference, the voice that one assumes to be the filmmaker's reports on his interaction with the caretaker of the church, who tries to stop their filming arguing that the ruin is dangerous. But, in the end, not only are they allowed to keep working, but the caretaker takes the opportunity to recount the history of the church during and after the Second World War, particularly its congregation's enthusiastic support of Hitler. The silence and avoidance of this monument rendered doubly fraught under the G.D.R. by its religious purpose in a state hostile to religion and by its erstwhile congregation's political stance, is now breakable. The first historical 'lesson' of the film then is the complex intermingling of continuity and change from 1933 to 1991, of movement and stasis.

But these opening minutes also establish the filmmaker's relation to his material and his audience. One watches the rest of the film knowing, or at least imagining, that the maker is American, knowing that he has a long-standing relation, and not an unproblematic one, to Berlin, but that he is also highly sensitive to, and desirous of representing, Berlin's seductive qualities. Eisenberg reveals nothing autobiographical, aside perhaps his nationality, and one doesn't learn until the credits at the end of the film that although that part of the script was almost certainly written by the filmmaker, the voice is not his but that of John di Stefano. It is as if he wants the viewer to know, from the beginning, something of from whence he comes, as a filmmaker, a theorist, a foreigner with a tie to Germany. But then he disappears again. That is not to say that the film becomes in any sense impersonal; Eisenberg's

Persistence, Daniel
Eisenberg, 2007

words reappear throughout the film—intertwined with those of Janet Flanner, Max Frisch, and Stig Dagerman. He is also perhaps, or perhaps not, the figure walking through the exhibition of romantic landscapes in the Schloss Charlottenburg, But we never hear again about the process of making the film or of interactions with those among whom the film is made.

Eisenberg orients us and then leaves us alone to grapple with what our eyes see and our ears hear, almost as if he's afraid that if we know too much, we'll prejudge too much, but he's nonetheless reluctant to disappear completely behind the camera. It is a fascinating presence/absence mirroring that of the titles of episodes of the film, as if he himself has no place here. This "here" is ambiguous. It is the here of Germany, the here of in front of, rather than behind, the camera, the here of what one hears in the soundtrack. The technical care and prowess of the film, however, mark his presence as definitively as writers mark theirs even when they choose not to use the first person. Let me echo in turn that gesture, although my version of reflexivity is a decidedly different one.

ABSENCE I: INTERIORITY IN RUIN

Striking in *Persistence* is the choice to limit the presence of interior spaces to the bureaucratic, institutional, or empty. The only non-destroyed interiors are those of the offices of the East German Secret Police (the Stasi), the laboratories in the Sachsenhausen concentration camp in which experimentation on human beings was carried out, and the exhibition space in the Schloss Charlottenburg. All are shown, furthermore, in their post-wall, museumified forms. The interior spaces of domesticity, of labor, of commerce, of prayer—whether in pre-war, ruined, Cold War, or post-wall forms—are all only present as absences. The historic footage—both Rossellini's and that produced by the U.S. Army Signal Corps—extensively used in the film, shows endless walls behind which there is nothing, an image echoed in Eisenberg's own footage of contemporary bullet-pocked, eroded, facades, behind which he never goes. The film is, in fact, full of window frames, many unglazed, bombed-out, some with glass and curtains. We never go into the homes, however, leaving one to wonder if in Eisenberg's vision there is no 'normal' interior space in this city and, perhaps, never was.

This comes in fascinating juxtaposition to two practices of Jews forced to leave their homes in Berlin and elsewhere in Europe in the 1930s and 1940s—the production of portraits of home, and the writing of restitution documentation when there was no hope of restitution—I have encountered in my own research.

Let me provide an example through the photograph album Bettina Roth gave to the archive now housed in the restored Neue Synagoge on Oranienburgerstrasse (also an important site in the film). Bettina Roth's early childhood home was in Berlin where her father worked as an international lawyer. In 1933 the family fled, abandoning their home in Dahlem for a new dwelling in England. Before leaving they, like substantial numbers of other bourgeois Jews, commissioned a photographer to memorialize that home. The family never returned to Germany but Bettina's

Fotoalbum Wohnhaus
von Rechtsanwalt
Dr. Ernst Frankenstein,
Berlin, Dahlem,
c. 1933. Geschenk der
Tochter Bettina Roth,
Neuilly-sur Seine.
copyright Stiftung
Neue Synagoge
Berlin-Centrum
Judaicum, Archiv.

Left and opposite:
Persistence

Left and opposite:
Persistence

parents proceeded to raise their daughters with the constant memory of the home and lives left behind. The photograph album that was the material heart of that memorialization traveled with their daughter to the suburb of Paris where she now lives and from thence, back to Berlin, to the Centrum Judaicum.

The photos in the album, seem, at first glance, a series of images of a typical enough bourgeois home, garden, and family in the Berlin of the early 1930s. One quickly realizes, however, that even if the home is not unusual, the photographs are. First of all, these photos are unusual in their quality. The images are beautifully, even lyrically, composed and lit, producing an ode to the house, a use of light and space not completely distant from that in *Persistence*. Like the film, leafing through the album takes one on an uncanny voyage between the present and past.

Secondly, they are almost all images of thresholds, standing in one place looking into another. In this they both echo many of the house portraits done on the eve of departure and parallel Eisenberg's camera's preoccupation with facades and the windows they hold. In these images, however, there are still two sides to the threshold, whereas in Eisenberg's the inside, the homeside, has been obliterated. But in the end, it may be Eisenberg's hollow structure that more accurately represents the exile's experience (if not the exile's hopes at the moment of departure). I think that this album may have come to mean so much to Bettina Roth not only for its capacity to recall a lost home—both in the sense of a physical dwelling and a nation— but also because it foreshadowed her sense of living liminally. After going into exile in 1933, she never returned to Germany, even to visit. As she put it when we talked in her current home in a suburb of Paris:

Every morning, every morning of my life for the last 73 years, my first impression as I start to wake up is that I am in my bedroom in Dahlem, the room that I was forced to leave, and to which I have never returned, never want to return, never can return. Each day commences with a cruel disappointment.

For Roth, her home is a synecdoche of her homeland and native city. After emigration to England where she learned to speak fluent English, she then made a life in Paris where she writes novels in French, but considers German her only real language. She has lived her post-war life psychologically on the margins, never fully in one place. She has never sought restitution or reparation moneys; rather she has been trying to give something back to Germany—the painful record of her life.

When I spoke with her about possible homes for the material remnants of her life, she replied that it absolutely had to go to an archive in Germany. When asked why— given that she has refused to ever return there, even for a brief visit—she replied somewhat obliquely, saying that her life had been a German life, and Germans would have to live with it. Yes, she had lived in England, she had lived in France, but that was incidental and fundamentally irrelevant. Her life-story was part of German-Jewish history, and it was to that community that, somehow, it should go, but said as she said it, this was if not a poisoned gift, then something close to it.

This bitterness resonates with both the present and absent interiors in *Persistence*. The exception to the generalization of the absence of 'normal' interiors in the film would seem to be the interior of the Schloss Charlottenburg. But the 1991–1992 exhibition space, in which the romantic landscapes with ruins (along with unbuilt landscapes) are displayed, is, as it works in the film, by no means normal leisure/cultural interior space. Our first view of the space is through the eye of a security camera with the simultaneous voice over providing first an account of account books, followed by what sounds like it could be a report of the observation of a spied upon subject, plausibly in G.D.R. times. The claustrophobic circle is closed when we see on the screen a painting of a woman standing in a window at the same time as the voice describes the object of observation walking to the window. A rushing truck provides a punctuation mark from the present and we are then launched into a reprise, in different terms, of the place of the past in the present.

Eisenberg takes us from the painted landscapes and ruins to Frederick the Great's constructed ruins in Sans Souci (his summer palace on the outskirts of Berlin, in Potsdam), describing Frederick's understanding that it was only through the contemplation of ruins that he could achieve real thought, as well as incrementally detailing (in dollars) the construction costs. The absurdity, if not obscenity, of paying to construct (and improve) ruins is highlighted first by a cut to the ruined façades of formerly East Berlin in the early 1990s, followed by the too-brightly colored footage of a devastated Braunschweig at the conclusion of the Second World War. Here Eisenberg wants to be sure we get it and the source and date of the military footage is provided. All of this echoes the very opening of the film (before the title) when we see Rossellini's frail, beautiful and too-thin, 13 year-old Edmund roaming through the ruins of Berlin in 1947.

Left: Petition and inventory filed for Mlle. Régine Casapus, 7 rue Ramey in Paris, French National Archives, Paris, Series AJ38, box, 5912, file D1

Right: Petition and Inventory filed by D1 Eugène Crémieux, lawyer, 17 place des Etats Unis, Paris, French National Archives, Paris, Series AJ38, box, 5912, file D1 Photographs: Leora Auslander

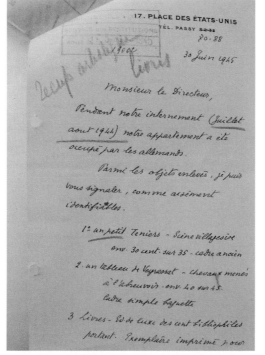

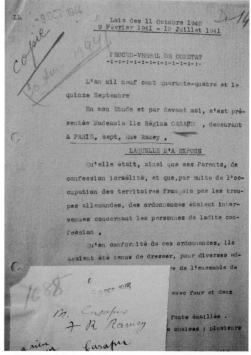

The result is a luminous view onto the gap between the late eighteenth and early nineteenth century romantic vision of ruins as something one actively and willfully constructs and the ruined state of Germany as a result of war. The film underscores the fact that events of the twentieth century rendered the romantics' vision of ruins hopelessly anachronistic. Aerial bombing, fire bombing, atomic bombing changed the meaning of ruin forever. But *Persistence* also underscores the fact that no vision of ruins adequate to the effects of mechanized war has been found. Rather, every effort in Germany has been, particularly in the post-unification period, to simply to erase the traces of destruction and with them memory of the violent regime that caused them. And yet, and this is one of the difficult paradoxes of this film, the footage of ruins, carefully framed by Rossellini, the American Army's camera men, or Eisenberg himself, is simultaneously almost unbearably beautiful and devastatingly painful. In that paradox Eisenberg suspends the viewer in a web of multiple temporalities, in multiple subject positions. We are at once with Frederick, contemplating broken buildings' aesthetic forms, and with Rossellini and the cameramen attempting to render the unbearable bearable through its aestheticization, and with the victims of twentieth-century violence, who experienced nothing but the brokenness. Finally, *Persistence* also underscores that it was the same civilization, albeit distant in time, that imagined romantic controlled ruins and that brought about complete ruin. Thus, the interior space of the Charlottenburg Schloss is in no sense "normal".

PROSPECT I: EVERYDAYNESS

The repeated shots of the Schloss' formal gardens, too, generate a sentiment of abnormal normality. Gardens are quintessential interior/exterior spaces, cultivated to produce a sense of domesticity, of comfort, of safety. They are nature tamed, even if they remain subject to its temporalities. Although domesticated spaces, they cannot, anymore than that other domesticated space, the home, provide protection against the events of the world. Thus, one of the voiceovers during a long shot of the gardens is the narration of end of the Soviet regime. All, visually, is still, peaceful, controlled, and out of time. And yet, that image in the viewer's eye is contradicted by what she hears, evoking both the complex dissonance of German experiences of the end of the Soviet Union, and the complex dissonance of the resumption of 'normal' life after Germany's defeat in the Second World War. Whether in the quite extraordinary shots of carefully-dressed women picking their way through the ruins of Berlin, or the beautiful boy roaming Rossellini's streets, or the streetcars running and cyclists riding calmly through devastated cities, ruined exteriors juxtaposed with tweeting birds, thriving trees, and the noises of trollies. Or the dissonance between the bright white of the newly painted window frames against the grimy walls in which they sit in Mitte in the years just following unification, the film conveys a sense of the necessity, perhaps inevitability, and amorality of life going on after the unthinkable has happened. This echoes the 'tone of voice' found in the petitions for restitution of the lost contents of homes of Jews returning to France in the fall of 1944. In these documents the authors move between grieving a lost life and the necessity of finding the means to continue life, with barely a pause.

In addition to the use of terrifying juxtapositions of everyday banality and catastrophe, Eisenberg lets nature do much of the work of reminding the viewer of the irrevocability of the passage of time, of the brutality of the rhythms of life.

The film is saturated with juxtaposed images of the natural and built environment. In stark contrast to the subjection of nature to human will represented by gardens, the trees, grasses, and bushes that spring up among ruins of churches, of homes, or of airforce bases are uncontrolled, untamed. In this context, the uncontrolled growth recalls the inexorability of nature, the triviality of human intervention and renders obscene the romantics' careful melding of constructed ruin and artificed landscape. The point was already made, but in case it had been missed, the corpses thrown haphazardly in indifferent green fields filmed by the U.S. Army forbids any escape from the harshness of this reality.

PRESENCE/ABSENCE/PROSPECT I: SIMULTANEITY

More disorienting even than the juxtaposition of the time of nature and the time of 'civilization' in *Persistence* is the different temporalities simultaneously heard and seen. Around minute 81 of the film, for example, the viewer is shown a statue of Marx and Engels sitting on Alexanderplatz in 1991–1992 at the same time as she hears a text from 1946. This is but one reprise of this technique through the film, a technique that is marked and unmarked. Often as one is listening and looking, the viewer and listener is not sure of whether she is currently in the late 1940s or the early 1990s; they seem disconcertingly the same. Eisenberg then provides the date or, the reference, comes that seems to clarify, to restore order. And yet the unnerving synchronicity remains, particularly when the text from one era seems to work so well with the image from another.

The reappearance of the gilded statue of Victoria atop the Siegessäule monument in the Tiergarten in Berlin reinforces this sense of the impossibility of the passage of time. The monument, inaugurated in 1873, served to commemorate German military prowess (including the annexation of Austria in 1938) and was restored in honor of Berlin's 750th birthday in 1987. It also of course, had a featured role in Wim Wenders' film *Wings of Desire* made in the same year. In Eisenberg's conjuring of the monument, its relation to both space and time becomes deeply puzzling. The viewer

Persistence

seems to be gazing at the Siegessäule while sitting in a fast-moving vehicle. And yet, the statue never moves out of view, the spectator never escapes, is never liberated from this iconic representation of Berlinness, of Germanness, unlike in Wenders' film, there is no happy ending, no love story. The spectator (or the city?) seems trapped in a high-speed stasis, perhaps in an effort to transcend, to overcome, the past that is impossible. In this context, attempting reconciliation through strategies of reconstruction and commemoration seem frail indeed.

PRESENCE AND ABSENCE REMEMBERING AND FORGETTING: MUSEUMIFICATION/MONUMENTALIZATION

Three of the most striking sequences, in a film with many such, are those in the Stasi headquarters/archives/museum and the Sachsenhausen concentration camp/museum and those around the ruins and reconstruction of the Neue Synagoge on Oranienburgerstrasse. These stretches of the film starkly pose the question/challenge of what can, what could, possibly come next after the willed destruction of two forms of neighborliness, of everydayness in Germany. The initial destruction came in the 1930s and 1940s with first the radical marginalization followed by the eradication of the German Jewish community. The second came in post-war East Germany when the security police set up an extraordinary system of spying and betraying within families, friendship circles and workplaces. In both contexts, albeit in very different ways and with differing consequences, fundamental human ties were consciously weakened to the point of destruction.

What happens next?

In Sachsenhausen and the Stasi headquarters, the sites of interrogation and terror have been preserved and transformed into museums. It has been assumed that the continued existence of the physical installations will somehow keep, and is essential to keeping, the memory of the dead alive. But Eisenberg undermines that hope/wish, first in the context of Sachsenhausen where the camera slowly pans the interior of the rooms in which human experimentation was carried out, but where now the visitor sees only surgical instruments/instruments of torture tidily arranged in class cabinets and the white-tiled operating/morgue tables have been thoroughly cleansed of blood, viscera, and screams. Unlike the visitor to the museum, the viewer of the film not only sees this space but also hears a voice read a letter to (one imagines) the filmmaker's mother on the occasion of her birthday in which he admits that he wants to know but doesn't/can't know what she lived through if not in this space then in one just like it.

The descendents, whether of the victims or the perpetrators, cannot bear to imagine what took place, what was experienced. Instead the sites are, and I use the word, again, obscenely preserved, to be visited in hopes of expiation, in the hopes of knowing while refusing to know.

The question of for whom one preserves emerged vividly a few years ago in the struggle over a suitcase. Pierre Lévi (who went by the name Leleu during the war) was a French Jew who was 44 years old at the time of his arrest, deportation, and death. He left a wife and two young sons who survived the war in France. His suitcase, bearing a label in his wife's hand, was recuperated by the Auschwitz-Birkenau Memorial and Museum. In 2005 that suitcase was very reluctantly loaned to the Foundation for the Remembrance of the *Shoah* in Paris, where it was identified by Pierre Lévi's son, Michel Lévi-Leleu, and granddaughter, Claire. Michel Lévi-Leleu was profoundly moved and shaken by this unexpected encounter with the valise he had last seen more than half a century ago as it accompanied his father on a trip that would end in Auschwitz. He found that he could not bear the idea that it would leave France, once again making that trip, but this time without his father. More hopeful that he would succeed in persuading the Auschwitz-Birkenau Museum to leave the suitcase on display in Paris than release it into private hands, he asked the Foundation to assist him in negotiations to that end. Those negotiations failed. The Museum refused to leave the valise in Paris on the grounds that it had an obligation to keep such objects in Poland, on the site of the camp, in order to bear witness to what had happened there. If the Museum were to allow survivors and heirs to reclaim or relocate these traces, they would risk denuding the Museum's collections thereby endangering its crucial mission. The Museum, in other words, defended its position on the grounds that it had a responsibility to "preserve the memory of the Holocaust", and that that preservation had to take precedence over the feelings of the victims' families.[4]

Faced with the continued demand that his father's suitcase return to Auschwitz, Lévi-Leleu filed a law suit in the French courts, settled only in June 2009. That settlement

Auschwitz suitcase by courtesy of the Auschwitz-Birkenau State Museum in Oświęcim

requires Lévi-Leleu to give up all claims in exchange for the suitcase's permanent loan to the Foundation.[5]

The Stasi headquarters are likewise preserved carefully under glass. Even the spot on what one imagines to have been the interrogator's desk where the varnish has worn off as the clerk's buttons rubbed against the surface as he handled file after file has been left intact. In the film, the telephone rings incessantly, unbearably, in the background as the camera pans the interior of the building and claustrophobia builds. Here the voiceover informs us of another impossible double-bind. Just as the preservation of Sachsenhausen appears to have been irresistible, so not only the Stasi building, but the files the building was designed to produce and generate have been kept, trapping those who produced and were recorded in them (very often the same people) in those sets of realities. Also calmly reported is just as Frederick the Great had trees cleared so that he could contemplate the ruins he had made to order at his castle at Sans Souci, so the head of the Stasi appropriated an office from which he could see and control all the comings and goings from the building. An eighteenth century fantasy of a relation of time and history collides with a twentieth century one.

Finally, and for me, most complicatedly, comes the reconstruction of the Neue Synagoge on Oranienburgerstrasse in Berlin Mitte (the same Mitte that appears early in the film *Absence I*, at minute 27:19 of the film). The synagogue was built in 1866 in the "Oriental style" to hold some 2,500 worshippers. It was largely destroyed by British bombing in 1943; most of what was left was torn down in 1953. Restoration was started by the East German government in 1988 and completed after unification in 1995. A decision was made to rebuild the most visible parts of the synagogue, particularly the spectacular golden dome, and to create the illusion from the street that the synagogue had, indeed, been returned to life. The inner walls and the remnants of the masonry of the actual synagogue were secured by a glass and steel structure. In fact, however, the building, despite the brave street-side facade, is a shadow of itself. The entire sanctuary is gone. The building now ends where, on the ground floor, the men prepared to enter the synagogue and on the second floor, where the women once sat to look down on the men below. The sanctuary is now laid out in stone in the empty space—partially protected by a glass roof—marking the dimensions of the destroyed section. Thus the scars left by history remain clearly visible behind the facade, to those who choose to engage the building and the institutions it houses.

Neue Synagoge, Berlin, Jüdische Gemeinde zu Berlin

Persistence

Parts of the old synagogue are once again used for prayer; an egalitarian minyan meets here. Other areas in the reconstructed building are used for the permanent and temporary exhibitions, as well as meeting space. The permanent exhibition recounts the history of the building and the lives it touched. It is housed in the old Vorsynagoge and visitors look out at the empty space behind. Included within the display are documents and objects that record Jewish life in Mitte.

The Centrum Judaicum that is the official record-keeper of Berlin's Jewish community and the modern addition to the synagogue that houses the archive also has classrooms where recent Russian Jewish immigrants learn German or study Yiddish or Hebrew, a small library for community members and the offices for everyday needs of the community. The archive's reading room is small—with five researchers it feels crowded—and most of those working are descendants of members of the community looking for their ancestors.[6]

Despite this activity, however, nothing can eradicate the truth (and horror) of the fact that the Nazi regime did succeed, if not eradicating Jewish life and culture from Europe, in decimating it so that anything Jewish that takes root here must necessarily be something else. Eisenberg juxtaposes the brave, bold, golden star atop the dome of the synagogue with the ruins, traces, and wanderings of the boy of Rossellini's film. (Wanderings excruciating in their loneliness even if one doesn't know that *Germany: Year Zero* ends with Edmund's suicide.) In conversation with Daniel Eisenberg he argued that this reading is too bleak; he asserted that the scene following this one is, in fact, redemptive. Leaving the synagogue we view archival footage depicting the Russian soldiers helping German women as they pick their way across the bombed-out cityscape. I have to admit that although I, too, find the scene both beautiful and moving, it doesn't counter-weigh the sense of void created elsewhere in the film.

Thus although here, unlike in the scenes of Sachsenhausen and the Stasi headquarters, there is the hope and desire of recreating life that, too, is ultimately, a forlorn hope.

PRESENCE II: MAKING FILMS AND WRITING HISTORY

Persistence raises fascinating questions concerning both the status/nature of evidence in the narrating of history, conceptions of citation, as well as of the differing capacities of the written word that is the conventional rhetorical device of the historian and of film, particularly avant-garde film that is not constrained by the narrative convention.

I, in my historical practice, move as Daniel Eisenberg does, between the present and past.[7] In this film there is a present of the written word, a present of the narrator's voice, a present of the sound effects, and of the images produced for this film. The past is present through historical film footage (of a variety of kinds), through historic words read aloud or shown on the screen. In historical writing, there is only the page (whether word or image). The narrating voice is necessarily in the present, the past makes its presence known through direct citation or embedded within footnotes. Historical narratives do not, generally, jar the reader as this film jars the viewer. Above all, historical narratives do not disrupt the sense of time as this film does; the past is safely in the past, the present in the present and time flows evenly. Here, because of the juxtaposition of kinds of images, as well as of sound, text, and image, the viewer never quite knows where she is in time and time seems to move at variable speeds.

So, what in the end, does "the historian" learn from this film? Can she enter into debate with it or build on its insights as she would a monograph? Are these even relevant questions? I think that they are although many would argue that there is nothing unusual about an artist addressing synchronicity, violence, traces. They might well ask, "Why take on the question of how this relates to history, to academic history? Why not just say that this a different genre? A different discipline?"[8] Taking *Persistence* seriously as a historical work throws into relief the limits of the academic discipline. It challenges the division between the aesthetic and the intellectual and the subjective and objective. It forces one to think about how seeing images is different from reading is different from hearing, how hearing words read aloud is different from seeing them written down, how listening to music is different from listening to a read text. It obliges one to think again about citation practices and what they're really about. It does more than challenge. *Persistence* demonstrates that attention to the situatedness of the historian and to the aesthetic and the affective is not in contradiction with the historian's mission of conveying as close as she can come to the truth of the past while being useful to the present. But these are generalities. *Persistence* also has much to teach historians about the specific historical problems it addresses.

Persistence is a remarkable history—and not just a primary source to be mined by historians—of Berlin in the early years after reunification, with much to say, as well, about the 60 preceding years. While conventional historians have written not only analytically sharp, but moving, histories of Berlin from 1933 to 1992, none can do the work of *Persistence*.[9] None can evoke the contrast between the drama of historical cataclysm and the seeming normality of everyday life as powerfully as *Persistence*. None can convey the effects of the layering of the events of the past in Berlin's material fabric, of Berlin as palimpsest, as effectively.[10] None can portray the simultaneity and intensity of the efforts of governments and individuals to both mask the past and to reveal it, the necessity (but perhaps also necessary failure) of the museumification of sites of horror. That difference is the difference between work that enables (or even obliges) its interlocutor to experience, synchronicity and unevenness in time and work that offers representations of temporal effects. It is through the work's aesthetic qualities—the texturing of sound and image as well as the cuts between historic and contemporary footage, as well as footage in various temporalities and through various angles of vision—that the film acts on the senses. This film transforms the experience, not only the understanding, of time and of history. *Persistence* thereby makes the continued presence, and linkages, of the Third Reich, the *Shoah*, the violence of the Second World War itself, the echoing violences of the Cold War and of the G.D.R. in the reunified city of 1992 visible. In that it is a brilliant history of the moment in which it was filmed.

THE PERSISTENCE OF THE ARCHIVE
THE DOCUMENTARY FICTIONS OF DANIEL EISENBERG

Scott Durham

"… I am well aware", Michel Foucault famously said of his excavations of the historical archive, "that I have never written anything but fictions".[1] The fictions Foucault recreates in his archaeologies are those of knowledge itself. In weaving the relations of what is said to what is seen—and so providing the frame within which it is possible to speak or show the truth within a given archaeological formation—these fictions form its archive. It is thus that Gilles Deleuze can write, à propos of Foucault's remark: "But never has fiction produced such truth and reality."[2] The viewer of Daniel Eisenberg's film *Persistence: Film in 24 absences/presences/prospects*, 1997, might be justified in inverting Deleuze's formula: "Never have truth and reality produced such fiction." For the documentary fragments, both historical and invented, of which this film is composed—images and voices excavated from distinct archaeological strata of the twentieth century's audiovisual history—appear before us as elements of a series of archives whose relations the viewer is called upon to imagine, in a multiplicity of provisional, overlapping or contending fictions that provide their successive frames. Early in *Persistence*, the film Eisenberg shot in Berlin in 1991 and 1992 in the wake of the collapse of East German Stalinism, the Stasi archive—considered as at once the enabling frame for observing and recording everyday existence and as the mythic object of collective fantasy—appears as a privileged site for such archival fictions:

Subject M opens letters at desk. 10 Minutes. Telephone rings. Subject answers telephone, gets up from desk, paces, returns to desk. See attached for transcript of conversation with G. Subject becomes animated. An argument seems to be in progress. Subject gets up from desk, paces, returns to desk, 3 minutes. Subject places phone down, walks out of room to kitchen, makes a cup of coffee, three minutes. Talks to self. See attached transcript….

... Subject M returns to desk, begins to write, 14 minutes. Subject M tears up paper and begins writing again, three minutes. Paces, sips coffee and begins to open mail, five minutes. M leaves room to toilet, two minutes... returns to room. Subject M returns to desk, begins to write. Somewhat agitated, subject scratches face, neck, scalp, three minutes. Subject walks to window, looks out three minutes....

"Persistence: Presence (III): Galerie der Romantik..." Schloß Charlottenburg (with instructions for viewing)

The scene evoked in this description—an imagined excerpt, read in voice-over, from an unnamed subject's file in the Stasi's archives—could almost be a fragment of Beckett. There is, as in Beckett's plays, the limitation of the field of action to a narrow frame. There is the way in which the permutation of the limited set of gestures and acts of speech observable within the borders of that frame (sitting down and getting up, pacing and scratching, exiting and returning, reading and writing, talking on the phone and talking to oneself) make visible, through their very limitation, a form of life—a possible world.

But there is also our awareness (sharpened by a title that helps frame this sequence for the viewer: "The Rules of Dispassionate Observation") that the character of this world as such is inseparable from its relation to an observer or narrator, who, like some of those in Beckett, is for some unknown reason obligated to record them. Indeed, the fact that these otherwise insignificant words and gestures, seemingly culled more or less at random from an individual life, appear to us as potentially meaningful turns in large part on the fact that they are given to us as already documented: "The files", as the voice-over reminds us, "would have to be selected, formulated, possibly dictated to a secretary...."

The documentation of the world imagined within this frame thus produces, at a stroke, the fiction of the larger frame in which we must place the existence of these documents: an archival fiction. This archival fiction—which begins with the assumption that there is nothing that can be done or said in a life, no matter how inconsequential, that is not subject to observation and documentation—calls upon us to imagine, not only the rooms where that life is lived, but the process of inscription by which the evidence of its existence is produced, the procedures according to which those documents are selected and preserved alongside those of other lives, and, finally, the space where such documents are assembled to be interpreted by a reader or viewer who, at the other end of this process, can oversee them only from a distance.

We are shown such a space near the end of *Persistence*: the suite of offices at Stasi headquarters formerly occupied by the G.D.R.'s last Minister for State Security, Erich Mielke, and his staff, offices which have now themselves been preserved as a museum. In the long takes and slow pans through which his camera surveys this space, Eisenberg, unlike the later film *The Lives of Others*, 2006, chooses not to emphasize the novelistic and sensationalistic aspects of the espionage and surveillance once headquartered here. Eisenberg emphasizes instead the ordinariness of these conference rooms and offices, with their austere East German modern furniture, whose monotony is only occasionally relieved by a plaster mask of Lenin or a potted plant.

Left and opposite:
Persistence

Of course, we cannot help but be aware throughout of at least one extraordinary fact about this space, methodically explored by Eisenberg's camera: the fact that it was in these otherwise ordinary rooms that a vast archive of everyday existence at the service of political repression would presumably have been evaluated and overseen—aiming, in principle, at the surveillance of an entire society (including the life of the fictitious Subject M). But we are also aware that the dramas that might have unfolded in these offices when they were at the point of the confluence of political power and social knowledge will remain forever invisible to us. And this makes it all the more striking that this center of surveillance, now that its professional observers have left their posts, has been preserved for all to see. The "archive of everyday observations" has itself become a museum, offered up for our own "disinterested observation", even as we are reminded by the insistent ringing of a phone that there are no longer any observers left to answer it.

Of course, neither the functioning nor the effects of these two regimes of observation— that of the apparatus of surveillance on the one hand and that of its museum on the other—are reducible to one another. As a museum exhibit, Stasi headquarters, in an abrupt historical inversion, is presented to us for the first time as an observable world. The rooms that frame the world in which Subject M has been observed, on the other hand, are never shown to us directly on screen, as a cinematic image. The voice-over reading of the documents describing M's life is juxtaposed instead with a series of documents from another archive, providing the frame for views of another nature. As we hear the narrative of M's movements, we are shown a visitor to an art museum, scrupulously observing a series of landscapes. This series of views

culminates in a painting representing another observer, seen from behind, who is herself contemplating the view of a landscape through a half-open window. As it turns out, we will return to this visit to the art museum later in the film. A shot of this same museum visitor, taken from behind as he contemplates a landscape (a shot which rhymes with the earlier shot of the observer represented in the painting), will serve as the prelude to the sequence on Stasi headquarters.

What implications might we draw from these juxtapositions? If the rooms where Subject M was observed are never shown to us directly—if that moment of his life is never given as a cinematic image, but only described by the film's voice-over—it might be argued that it is because M's life, as an invention of the film, is fictive, whereas the space of this museum exhibit is an artifact of history which can appear before us as a visible and documentable reality. But this difference, between the invisibility of a fictive world and the visibility of a historical actuality, is perhaps less important than what both have in common: the fact that neither can exist except as an artifact of the archive, historical or fictive, in which it has been recorded and preserved. As with the views of landscapes preserved for our contemplation in museums, we have access to only those views of M's life that have been documented and selected by those assigned to observe him. This is the archival fiction that frames our view of Subject M: If this fragment of M's existence is to be preserved after the fall of the Stalinist regime, it can only be as an exhibit in a "museum of everyday observations" capable of outlasting the world of observer and observed alike.

The monuments of East German Stalinism, both visible and invisible, were being dismantled all around Eisenberg as he was shooting footage for *Persistence*. Of the film's sequences devoted to the disappearance of the G.D.R., one of the most striking images is one that, in the hands of another filmmaker, might well have been a mere cliché: the image of a colossal statue of Lenin as it is being taken down. Such images, from the toppling of the statue of Czar Alexander III in Eisenstein's *October*, 1928, to that of the statue of Saddam Hussein as seen on CNN, have become emblematic of revolutions and "regime changes" of every sort, regardless of their particular political valence. For, in such cases, the overturning of a monument, as the figure for the overthrow of a regime, allows us to imagine the transformation of a political or social order as a single punctual event that might take place before our eyes.

But Eisenberg approaches this familiar trope of films of revolution and counter-revolution from another angle, portraying the removal of this monument, not as an immediately graspable image, but as a laborious process of disassembly that unfolds slowly over the duration of the film. Early in *Persistence*, we see the statue still intact, although it is largely ignored by passers-by, except by a small group posing for a photograph in front of it. (Are these tourists, one wonders, or locals, aiming to preserve their image alongside this icon already condemned to disappear?) A bit later in the film, we see workers assembling scaffolding rod by rod, as they prepare to take down the colossus. A sparse and casual crowd looks on, the murmur of their conversations occasionally broken by the ring of hammers on metal as the scaffolding is assembled around the monument, as if it were the task of these workers to provide a last frame through which the towering figure of Lenin might be viewed. It is only very late in the film that we see this statue again, this time almost completely obscured by the structure that has grown up around it, its massive head having at long last been removed from its still-imposing torso. But within that provisional

October: Ten Days That Shook the World, Sergei Eisenstein, 1927

Left and opposite:
Persistence

structure, which had to be constructed in order for his image to be dismantled, this relic of a half-unmade social order still remains discernible. As with the abandoned Soviet air force base on which Eisenberg's camera also lingers—taking the time to register the full effect of its broken shells of helicopter cockpits and decaying jet engines piled up as if in some abandoned lumber yard of the Cold War—it will yet require a long and patient labor for its remains to be removed.

But if this is so for the G.D.R.'s statues and edifices, how much more is it the case for the less visible architecture created by the old order with which we began: the "archive of everyday observations" left behind by the Stasi? For the effects of that persistent archive turn less on the monuments visible from outside it than on the forms of observation by which the archive makes its subjects visible within its frames. No doubt the monumental scale of the enterprise, as with the statue, is a part of the Stasi's legend:

That the index alone for the files was 1.2 kilometers long, that the files themselves were 200 kilometers [...] that the buildings were so heavy and overloaded that they were sinking into the ground, that a water-pressure ballast system was needed to shore up the structures.

But as imposing as the edifice containing them might appear, the real power of these archives turns on the effects they continue to produce after the historical world they document has seemingly been erased from the landscape. These effects are first of all felt at an individual level, as when the arc of an individual life, seen retrospectively within the frame of this archival space, is reevaluated by the one who lived it.

We routinely open your mail, tap your phone, bug your apartment. You won't know when you'll be surrounded by "informal collaborators", some of them your closest friends. One day you'll find out that you yourself have a name—forked tongue, top-drawer, ivory tower.... That you too are a collaborator, whether you know it or not... whether you like it or not....

But it is above all at the collective level that the effects of the archive outlive the institutions that gave rise to them:

On the night of November 9th people barricaded themselves inside in order to protect the files.... They immediately formed a citizen's committee with the express purpose of watching over the files until a time when their safety could be guaranteed. People ate, slept, perhaps made love among the files. And from that moment on the files became a national obsession, providing a standard to which everyone was held. As before, everyone became enslaved by the files... though now for different, if equally dark purposes. Someone said, "Our obsession with the files reduced us to using the standards of the Stasi to judge ourselves, leaving it to them, once again, to decide who is with us and who is against us."

The voice-over recounts how a group of citizens, having made the commitment to protect the files that had documented the lives of a whole society, ironically creates something like an image of social life in miniature within the interstices of the archive itself. And if this image stays with us long after the film is over (even though, like the 'views' of the life of Subject M, it is never shown to us directly), it is perhaps in part because the ultimate meaning of this commitment is ambiguous. Should this occupation of the files be interpreted as a symbolic act, even as a utopian image, as the detail of making love among the files seems to suggest? Are we witnessing a sort of "be-in" among the files, through which the collective enacts a new form of life in the space in which its old life had been recorded? Or is this occupation rather to be understood, as the voice-over suggests, as the symptom of a collective investment in the files as a privileged site of political and moral truth—an investment so deep-seated among those that had been observed that even the most ardent opponents of the regime find themselves unexpectedly unable to give it up? In either case, *Persistence* shows us how this archival fiction still haunts the ruins of East German Stalinism, weighing (to borrow Marx's phrase) "like a nightmare on the brains of the living"—the fiction of a life lived entirely within the space of its own archive.

There is a sense in which this image of a life within the Stasi archives can be said to have imposed itself upon the filmmaker as the result of a historical contingency. It may be that, as Eisenberg worked on what would become *Persistence* in 1991–1992 the ways in which the old forms of life and evidence persisted in this moment of historical passage alongside and within the new—both as a documentary reality and as a

Persistence

collective representation or myth—became most immediately graspable in the realized fiction of a life completely circumscribed by the organization of archival space. It may also be that this archival fiction could only become fully visible as such once its frame had been broken by the historical crisis itself, and its fragments assembled alongside those of other archives, both real and virtual, haunting the German landscape. In any case, the Stasi files constitute only one of the multiple archaeological strata that are excavated by Eisenberg in *Persistence*. We have seen how the imagined observations recorded in the Stasi archives are juxtaposed with the "views" preserved within the art museum—an archival space that is itself framed by its relation to the museum that the Stasi headquarters has become. Elsewhere in the film, these various officially sanctioned archives are placed in relation to a broader field of documents and artifacts, all of which may be imagined as elements of an archive yet to be assembled, and which it is the task of the filmmaker to excavate and reconstruct.

A partial list of such elements would include the color footage shot by the Signal Corps cameramen in the ruins of Berlin in 1945–1946, and those same ruins as re-imagined in Rossellini's roughly contemporaneous neorealist fiction, *Germany: Year Zero*, 1948. But it would also include the record Eisenberg himself creates of the traces of wartime and prewar life that remain inscribed on the landscape of Germany as it confronts another historical break, with the end of the Cold War. In this footage, *Persistence* revisits spaces laden with historical significance, such as the abandoned Elisabethskirche with which the film opens—a church which the voice-over tells us Hitler himself is said to have promised to rebuild for its loyal congregation, but the ruins of which had remained untouched and unacknowledged by Berliners since the war. It also would include, as if in counterpoint, the ruined synagogue, whose community was exterminated by the Nazis, which we see under reconstruction at the end of *Persistence*. These images resonate powerfully with the ruins of Rossellini's post-war Berlin, with which they are intercut, as well as with Eisenberg's own footage of the soon-to-be-dismantled monuments of a disappearing G.D.R..

But Eisenberg's camera also assiduously documents images and artifacts whose exhibition and narrative value is less obvious, such as the images of burnt out and abandoned Jewish shops, apparently unoccupied since the war, or the haunting images of vanished buildings whose traces on surviving structures are made visible by the discerning eye of our cinematic archivist. In his treatment of the latter set of images, Eisenberg, as Jeffrey Skoller has remarked, makes visible the "ghostly outline" of an earlier stratum in the history of Berlin—a work he carries out with the vigilance and skill of a paleographer deciphering the underwriting of a palimpsest.[3]

Persistence may thus best be understood as an archive of archives, which at once constitutes a new archival space of its own and invites us to interrogate the relations between archival formations, and the narratives associated with them. In this, *Persistence* both returns to and reformulates the problems explored in the two previous films of Eisenberg's post-war trilogy, each of which has, as its organizing principle, a distinct archival fiction. *Displaced Person*, 1981, stages the fictive constitution of the archive as such—an archive that, however, produces effects of truth only by weaving fictive relations between its documentary elements. There is no immediate historical relation between the newsreel images of Hitler's triumphant tour of Paris and the unattributed and unlocalized found footage of two boys on a bicycle, with which it is repeatedly intercut in this short film. If these two boys who gaze back at us from a vanished world—who were not filmed, as it turns out, in wartime Paris, but in New York before the war—can nonetheless, through this juxtaposition, come implicitly to serve as figures for the innumerable refugees and deportees displaced by the war alluded to by Eisenberg's title, it is only because this document of their childhood has itself been 'displaced' from its point of origin by the very cinematic archive in which their image is preserved.

In the next film of the trilogy, *Cooperation of Parts*, 1987, it is seemingly for his own origins that Eisenberg's camera searches, seeking to make visible the inaccessible past world of his parents. (Survivors of the *Shoah* and Soviet labor camps, his parents met as 'displaced persons' in the aftermath of the war, making Eisenberg, in the most immediate biographical sense, a product of the war's catastrophes.)[4] The archival fiction of this film no longer foregrounds, as does *Displaced Person*, the constitution and articulation of archival space as such. The focus of *Cooperation of Parts* is, rather, on the attempt of the author/investigator to document an experience uncontainable within its archival frame, a documentary project indissociable from his desire to feel on his "own skin" the effects of a primal scene at once familial and historical. But the forms through which this pursuit of origins is documented, while making vividly felt the intensity of the documentarian's desire to resurrect an image of the past, seem nonetheless intended to foreground the way in which the pursuit of this desire reorients—and at times disorients—our experience of the present.

Perhaps most striking in this regard are the destabilizing effects of Eisenberg's erratic camera movements, as when the camera, in a sequence framed by the filmmaker's journey to Dachau, follows a floating piece of ash in its twisting descent, only to seek out, in a series of abrupt and disjointed close-ups, the place where it might have come down. In the last shots of this sequence, we seem almost on the verge of seeing, in footage that documents little more than patches of grass seen in extreme close-up, the last remains of the lives that had once been inscribed, "in calcium and phosphorus", on the earth that grass has overgrown. But like that piece of ash—which is only perceptible for the brief interval in which it drifts before becoming indistinguishable from the new background in which we must attempt to rediscover it—the image of the past appears to its present pursuer in *Cooperation of Parts*, not with the fixity and immobility of a document, but as a fleeting movement that our eye must pursue on the edge of the perceptible world. Because it emanates from an inaccessible past world, that image is unrecognizable to us in the present, appearing out of focus or out of kilter with our current frame of reference. As with the photographs of the narrator's parents that should document that past—images which are only evoked by their descriptions in voice-over, as the virtual doubles of the documentary images of the present that appear in their place (as when the photograph of the mother parting with friends from a German train station in 1948 is described over contemporary footage of a train station in France)—the image of the past in *Cooperation of Parts* appears above all as a perturbation in the image of the present: as a latent or virtual image, that becomes visible only at the limits of what we are capable of seeing.

In *Persistence*, the third film of the trilogy, Eisenberg develops an archival fiction distinct from the other two: that of the historical crisis, in which one archaeological formation breaks apart and gives way to another. *Persistence* does not stage the constitution of the archive as such, as does *Displaced Person*, nor does it follow *Cooperation of Parts* in attempting to resurrect and document an experience that exceeds what is visible or articulable within the world we inhabit. And yet there is a sense in which this last archival fiction reframes and illuminates the others, by imagining a single space in which the ruins of multiple archaeological formations coexist: an archive of archives. In shattering the existing archival frame, the historical break makes visible new dimensions in its documentary elements as we follow their passage from one archaeological formation to the next. As we have seen, the dissolution of the G.D.R. and its system of surveillance does not only lay bare the archival frame underlying one form of social knowledge: it makes it possible for the filmmaker to excavate the multiplicity of archaeological strata that compose the German cultural landscape, and to see how (and with what effects) documents and images, having been dislodged from the ruins of one archive, find themselves, like the found images of *Displaced Person*, reassembled and reinterpreted within another. Conversely, with his ingenious appropriation of footage from *Germany: Year Zero*—where the gaze of Rossellini's young Edmund, through the use of match-cutting, appears at various points in *Persistence* to fall upon images of contemporary Germany, even as he explores the rubble of post-war Berlin—Eisenberg dramatizes in a different way the disorienting effect, so central to *Cooperation of Parts*, of moving beyond the limits of one's own historical frame.[5]

But in *Persistence*, unlike in the two preceding films, this abrupt leap ahead in time—and with it, the unexpected passage of the protagonist, without leaving the same space, between historical worlds—is pictured as the folding of one incomplete archival frame upon another. Edmund moves from the broken frames of the ruins of post-war Berlin (with its precarious skeletal structures as filmed by Rossellini and the Signal Corps) to the provisional frames of the scaffolding shot by Eisenberg in post-G.D.R. Berlin (within which the monument to Lenin is disassembled, and around which its abandoned synagogue is to be rebuilt.) When Edmund's gaze leads us, in its exploration of the layers of the city's history, across the gap between historical worlds, this leap in time is thus not imagined as a plunge into the unknown, but (as elsewhere in *Persistence*) as a series of deframings and reframings, in which the landscape we thought we knew is remapped from one historical break or crisis to the next, obliging us to imagine a new place for ourselves within it.

To imagine the leap from one world to another is not, in itself, to invoke the utopian promise of the *novum*. No doubt, as we have seen in Eisenberg's treatment of the Stasi archives, the dream of utopia is not excluded from this movement of reframing. But, when such a wish appears, it can only be formulated as a utopia of the archive, where the transformation of social relations is imagined through a reappropriation and reordering of its documents and monuments.

We are given a language for expressing such a wish in the last sequence of the film. A group of adolescents casually climbs and leans upon a monument to Marx and Engels in what was once East Berlin, posing for the cameras of their friends as they take a moment to document their visit for some future archive. In the last shot, we read, scrawled in spray paint on the back of the monument, a comic post-Stalinist reinscription: "Next time, everything will be better."

This wish expressed only tentatively and self-mockingly, does not project a life beyond the archive. Rather, like the new life of the collective occupying the Stasi archives, it flashes up in the space between its frames—in the gap between the monuments of the past and a future archive, where the meaning of those monuments will have been rewritten. In *Persistence*, it is thus not only the space of our historical disasters, but also the trajectory of our dreams, that assumes the forms of the archival fictions that envelop us. In the shadow of those fictions, we pass from document to document, from monument to monument, and from frame to frame, like the denizens of Borges' Library of Babel.

Persistence

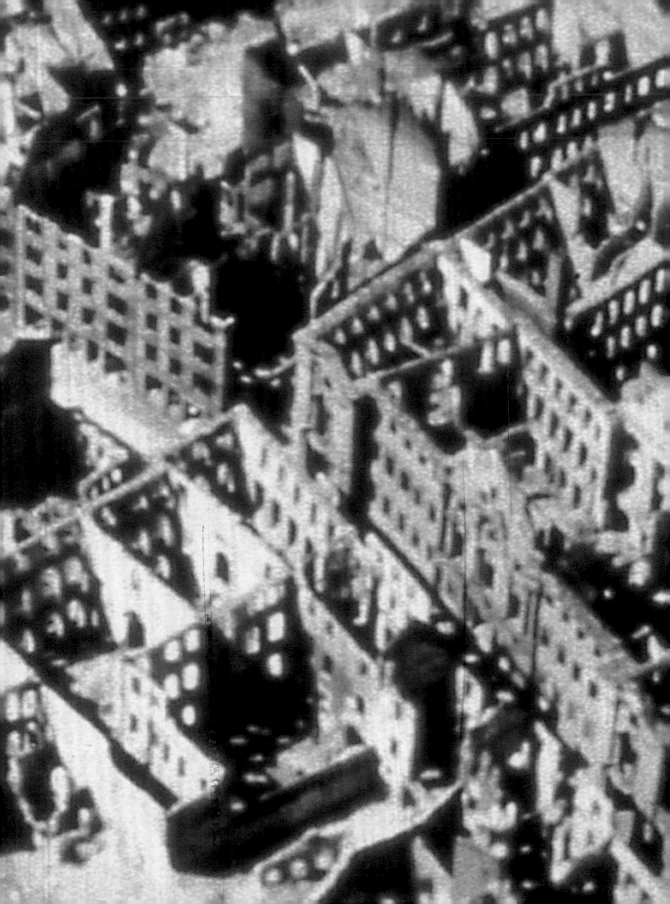

NON-PLACES, NOMADS AND NAMELESS ONES
NOTES ON *SOMETHING MORE THAN NIGHT*

Christa Blümlinger

Something More Than Night, Daniel Eisenberg, 2003

Kies und Geröll. Und ein Scherbenton, dünn, als Zuspruch der Stunde. Augentausch, endlich, zur Unzeit. [Gravel and rubble. And a shard-tone, thin, as the hour's solace. Barter of eyes, finite, untimely Night.]
Paul Celan, *Nacht* [1]

Daniel Eisenberg's work is marked by its fragmentary forms. It's as if places and images—each with their own pictorial energy and capacity for multiple articulations—were formed into a constantly changing array of combinations. The montage presents each scene as a reversible, variable segment, and sets into motion manifold analogies, connections, and associations.

In *Something More Than Night*, 2003, this aesthetic of the fragment takes shape from a controlled number of seemingly disparate documentary scenes in the form of more than 70 views of night in a large American city. This is a film conceived from the center outward, one which, despite its linear series of scenes, appears to have neither beginning nor end. Its construction can be described by the principle of "cartography", as formulated by Gilles Deleuze and Félix Guattari, and is laid out rhizomatically like a structure with several entrances and exits, and multiple axes. [2]

Most of the time, the camera is set up outdoors, in a stationary position outside lighted windows, doors, and entryways, but also on traffic arteries, broad plazas, bridges, and in large interior spaces. Its position is often separated from the scene observed by almost invisible glass partitions, by gratings, by protruding walls, or an atmospheric veil. The camera's perspective is rarely elevated, (like that of a video surveillance camera) it's more often like that of a pedestrian standing in the middle of traffic. We're reminded of its location in the city's flow by the temporary darkening and blurring caused by the appearance of figures or objects suddenly intruding into the foreground between the camera and the main action. At times the view is blocked. Pedestrians and vehicles

repeatedly introduce new relationships into the visual space with their shifting outlines, surfaces, and lines of movement.

The film is a virtual walk through the city. It is in several places at once, yet it doesn't purport to be everywhere. This Man with a Movie Camera is not so concerned with the rhythms of the electrified city as with the mystery of a moment drawn from the duration of a single shot. It's in the waiting, that our attention to the visual density of a composition is sharpened; to the figures and objects, and to the division of spaces. But waiting also sharpens the senses for the smallest occurrences, peripheral movements, and otherwise barely visible activities. It is precisely the duration of the shots that allows for the development of imaginary worlds on the margins of fiction. Eisenberg is not as closely related to Vertov as to his contemporary, Chantal Akerman, who, between her film essay *News from Home*, 1976, and her feature film *Toute une nuit*, 1982, developed a sensual method for showing night in the metropolis as a space of possibilities.

The first shot is emblematic. In it, we see part of the glass exterior wall of an office, symmetrically divided by the vertical line of a supporting beam. Behind half-opened blinds on the left stands a man facing idly outward; on the right, a woman facing inward is busying herself at her desk. She moves back and forth into the man's space until he exits, passing behind another, opaque glass wall, where he is only visible in silhouette. Only then does the woman stop her pacing. She makes a telephone call. This scene lasts about three minutes. It is one of the few fragments in the film that is continued

Left and opposite:
*Something More
Than Night*

later, though not for five more shots, at which time the light in the office is turned off
and the woman also leaves the room and walks down the corridor behind it, offering the
camera a shadow play of her own. This reprise points up the virtual nature not only of the
duration of the first shot, but also of its location: as a fragment, it could just as well be
placed somewhere else in the film. But picking up the scene a second time also points to
the idea of simultaneity on which this big-city film is based. Between the man's exit and
the woman's there are four shots showing others at work somewhere in the evening city,
in glass office towers or as security guards in palatial, transparent lobbies.

To classify *Something More Than Night* as a film about Chicago by night would be off
target, because the city being filmed here is barely identifiable by its architecture,
and it's precisely not about what we normally mean by "nightlife". The film is also
not an essay about places in the modern metropolis in Baudelaire's sense, where
the historical, identifiable places are still part of the city's reference points or places
of memory. Here it is primarily a matter of a city's non-places, as described by
Marc Augé, taking up Michel de Certeau's idea of the anonymous passageways and
transit points of our "supermodern" age: air or rail lines, freeways and modes of
urban transportation (airplanes, trains, buses), as well as airports, railroad stations,
large hotel chains, theme parks, or wholesale supermarkets. Augé uses the term
to denote a world of provisional transit sites, "where the habitué of supermarkets,
slot machines and credit cards communicates wordlessly, through gestures, with
an abstract, unmediated commerce"; in short: a world "surrendered to solitary
individuality, to the fleeting, the temporary and ephemeral".[3] Most of the time,

*Something More
Than Night*

it is just such locations that we see in *Something More Than Night*. Even the film's title suggests another dimension of these urban passageways: the temporal, often immeasurable space of night, the "untimely", as Paul Celan calls it.

In this film many people can be seen variously moving along, or waiting to move along, in the dead of night. A harsh, greenish fluorescent light shines in the waiting areas, at the ticket counters, and above the conveyor belts at airports. The waiting people settle in as best they can, resting in a wheelchair, sitting down to read in the shade of a potted plant, or standing in line. In the just as brightly lit supermarket, everyone is occupied with their shopping. But outside, at bus stops and subway stations, or perhaps in less well-lighted foyers and public gardens, there is occasionally some gesture that declares the non-place off limits. One body suspends the unwritten law of anonymity by turning to another body as if they were in different surroundings.

In one wide-angle shot, we see a network of gray concrete piers in a parking garage with a spotlight shining in the center. A young couple stands in the shadow of one pier, when suddenly a car approaches, seeming to frighten them away. The camera waits until the next passerby comes into view. Another time, the camera pans to follow the movement of two men cleaning a wooden balustrade in a public garden. In one of the rare connected sequences in the film, a shift in the scale of the shot is initially used to emphasize the proximity to figures who are working and simultaneously conversing. But soon a bright spotlight, reflected off a light stone surface, blocks our view, and the scraps of conversation blend together with the ambient urban noise. Whenever there is any intimacy between persons, or between persons and the camera, it is always brief.

In the transitory non-places no one is ever really alone. Now and then, relationships and identities develop as in a palimpsest, a phenomenon that Michel de Certeau calls the "invention of the everyday" and which he locates at the interface of abstract place and concrete space. The transformation of a (non-)place into a space "in relation to a milieu" is not only possible, but is practiced daily, in a continuous negotiation with the constantly changing group of people in one's surroundings.[4] In order to grasp the phenomenon of the contemporary world of passages, Marc Augé in turn, proposes a distinction that derives the non-place precisely from practical spatial experience. First of all, Augé differentiates between the symbolized, anthropological place and the non-symbolized, modern or "supermodern" non-place. Secondly, he sets the firmly circumscribed space of one place against the fragmented, mobile space of the traveler through places as the archetype of the non-place.[5]

In Eisenberg's film we can see both in Certeau's sense the transformations of places into spaces or spaces into non-places , but also in Augé's sense the interchangeability and transience of non-places. This is evidenced by prescriptive, functional signs, or by means of a standardized architecture. Above all it appears as the solitary activity of the "supermodern" consumer. At broad toll plazas, the drivers wait, lined up at dozens of booths, until they're given the green light and allowed to pass. Long after the evening rush hour, huge filling stations await the occasional late customer with dozens of self-service pumps standing ready in the bluish light. The architecture of a large retail outlet, where people serve themselves from six-foot-high shelves, bears witness to an army of consumers. Everywhere a digital language of ciphers and codes signals access to information, while customers hear special offers over the store loudspeakers. We are in the age of a "control society" in which the masses are recast as data and markets (Gilles Deleuze).[6] Or, in Augé's terms, there are two complementary but distinct realities in this film: "spaces formed in relation to certain ends (transport, transit, commerce, leisure)" and "the relationships that individuals have with these spaces". This distinction, according to Augé, does not exclude connections; on the contrary, it allows for the analysis of mediated, purpose-oriented communication in non-places: "As anthropological places create the organically social, so non-places create solitary contractuality."[7] The film illustrates this solitude not only in its images, but also through the fragmentary form of the montage.

The scale of the shots varies among the fragments. One time, the camera directs our eye-level view toward a row of what might be thought of as theatrical dioramas joined together into a single gigantic structure. With views into the cubicles of illuminated, transparent office towers, the logic of reduplication in glass-and-steel architecture is graphically visible. When the camera is set up at ground level, it calls our attention to the alignments of a building, such as the connection between two parallel boulevards as viewed through the revolving doors of a spacious lobby, for example. It is precisely in the passageways of "supermodern" architecture that a rational order of the visible is reflected. Thus the transparent construction of airports allows us to observe its structure on several levels. We see how the arrangement of people standing in line at counters follows a metal barrier whose function it is to control bodies within a space.

Left and opposite:
*Something More
Than Night*

The architectural settings are also presented as a matter of proportion in *Something More Than Night*. This is especially and emphatically apparent in a loose series of shots in which the majestic lobby of a train station is framed.[8] The first thing we see, from a high angle diagonal point of view, is a section of the light-colored marble floor from which three enormous double benches of dark-brown wood stand out like sculptures. Only when two young men cross the visual field do we get some idea of the dimensions, not only of the long benches, but of the entire lobby as well. Another shot shows the same lobby in a normal view and focuses in closer on one of the benches. At one end of it we see a man lying stretched out and another on the other end sitting upright, dozing. Voices stand out against the indefinable background noise, their reverberations again suggesting the vast size of the space. Finally a third view, a kind of counter long shot, frames the seated man from one side. From this angle we are able to see the other side of the bench, where someone has also laid down to rest. In between the sleepers and the camera passersby occasionally cross the field of vision. We see the diverse relationships practiced within a given space, used by some as a place to sleep, by others as an anonymous transit zone.

A very different kind of motion-event, one that also brings relationships of scale into play, is shown in a fragment filmed at a church facade. In a lengthy still shot we see a stone cross with the figure of Christ enthroned under neogothic arches; then finally we discover the source of a squeaking sound: a small lift rolls down through the frame to lower a man who is apparently restoring or cleaning the building. This kind of cleaning work is done at night, and as much as possible, out of sight. The film uses a number of such entrances, not only to indicate the gigantic dimensions of a space but also to show the huge expanse of surfaces whose maintenance requires a considerable amount of time. Ingo Kratisch's precisely placed and usually stationary camera pans now and then to emphasize this spatial-temporal dimension of work. Thus, in one of Chicago's grand lobbies, we follow the movement of a cleaning woman sweeping with a wide broom from the regal staircase toward the exit. The angle widens with her movement, lights are reflected on the stone floor, and in the background a large glass revolving door provides an unobstructed view of the street. While we saw the woman's work in a different context in the preceding shot, i.e., as a parallel activity to those passing the time playing arcade games in an adjacent room, now the motion of the camera indicates the actual function of the lobby, as a place of passage.

The rare pan of the camera usually functions to point out connections between interior and exterior, architecturally determined passageways and virtual lines of movement, or transportation linkages, like that between a terminal and a Greyhound bus. The camera also pans, functioning as a montage of two elements, at the end of a series of three shots in a steel factory. The foundry hall, a structure from the modernist period, is open on several sides, and we see it from just outside one of the doorways. The spectacle of blazing light, from which a worker is taking his break, is linked by the camera's movement to the white headlights of passing cars. This linking of interior and exterior occurs not only as a demonstration of two different, parallel light sources working at the level of visual composition; it also refers to the superimposed urban noise. Throughout the film, the synchronous sound accentuates the background traffic noise to which the city is constantly subjected.

*Something More
Than Night*

Something More Than Night takes us into an intermediate world between dream and reality, to the threshold of other, invisible settings. The camera is set up not only to record the nocturnal spaces and parallel worlds of a city, but also to give access to figurations of simultaneously expressive and enigmatic depth. There is a paratactic, associative form beneath the surface that connects Eisenberg's film with Celan's poetry.[9] Its fragmentary form has at once a personal and a historical horizon, namely that of the concentration camps, displacement, and emigration. Daniel Eisenberg, unlike Celan, belongs to the second generation; he owes his existence to the fact that his parents survived.[10] His questioning bears the mark of his parents' trauma. Poetically enigmatic in *Displaced Person*, 1981, compressed and more explicit but just as fragmented and repetitive in *Cooperation of Parts*, 1987, this is clearly the project of the following generation. In *Something More Than Night*, we can observe a poetics of rupture, albeit one whose horizon is no longer explicitly decipherable. In his fragmentary, associative form, Eisenberg develops a logic of the non-place without the anthropological dimension that could create the "organically social".

The poetic alignments of the film load the present day with virtual, past, and simultaneously inaccessible images. This is demonstrated in the expressive exterior shots of Chicago's skyscrapers: facades shot diagonally from a low angle, their lights fading in fog; or geometrically constructed ensembles of high-rises standing out against the midnight blue of the sky, their windows like a firmament filled with tiny, inaccessibly distant lights.[11] With such randomly placed fragments, the film touches on other time-spaces. Almost every scene in this film reads like a picture puzzle; some are like hieroglyphs. Eisenberg's night has something of Celan when the latter says "Flutender, groß-/zelliger Schlafbau.//Jede/Zwischenwand von/ Graugeschwadern befahren." ("Flooding, big-/celled sleepyard.// Every partition overrun/ by squadrons of gray.")[12]

On the other hand, despite all its inhospitality, *Something More Than Night* repeatedly derives a virtual beauty from Chicago's non-places. Now and then a utopian dimension sets in above the arrangement and duration of scenes, a dimension we could call, in Michel Foucault's terms, "heterotopia", an "other" space—understood as a "simultaneously mythic and real contestation of the space in which we live".[13] One such mental view is conveyed most emphatically in a doubled framing that places the brightly lit interior of a truck in the center foreground like a proscenium stage in the midst of nighttime street traffic.[14] The rear door stands open, the truck's hazard lights are flashing, and two men have set themselves up at a table inside, as if in a workshop. The elevated tracks run overhead, above the truck; other vehicles roar by on either side.

Another time, the daily ritual of waiting in traffic offers us an event created out of a visual riddle and its eventual solution. At first, we see just a steel structure in a medium long shot, and a bell rings off camera. Then suddenly the image begins to move, a steel walkway comes into view, the surface facing the camera is lowered, and we have a clear view into the distance. The stage we see now is completely transformed, and pedestrians appear on it. The theatricality of the night presents itself to the meandering, strolling eye of the camera, unprompted. Perhaps the clearest example of this occurs in a virtually choreographed scene where a man and a woman are practicing shadowboxing behind the inviting windows of a fitness studio.

A preformed mythological heterotopia is offered in those moments, linked to Walter Benjamin's notion of arcades, as when the camera stops in front of lighted display windows, fashion boutiques, photographers' studios, or even snack bars, each time framing the exterior and allowing cars and pedestrians to cross in between. The film's fragments develop a figurative and compositional system of correspondences through the straightforward arrangement of all these objets trouvés of ordinary life at night. The "beauty" of each of the shots lies not only in a keen sense of duration, but also in a pictorial ordering of light, color, space, and line. Eisenberg shows the parallel worlds of night not just through variations on the contrast of bright interior and dark exterior; but also by emphasizing several levels of the image. Depth of field shows the simultaneity of foreground and background, but so do pictorial compositions emphasizing the perspective, or perhaps the focal point. With the framing of entry arches, doors, and windows, we gain insights into, or outlooks onto night, always suggesting a somewhere else, somewhere behind, somewhere beyond that we cannot see. Rarely are we offered a direct, unimpeded view as a "window on to the world". The camera looks, if not across the thresholds of buildings, then through gratings and fences, or out from behind protruding walls. When on one occasion the camera seems to be observing directly, watching men in a gym who are themselves looking through another window, the reflections in the glass panes suggest the distanced, ephemeral viewpoint of the nocturnal flâneur.

In these sensual studies of a city after dark, something like a school of perception develops, in which the proximity, emptiness, or closure of figurative groupings are of

Something More Than Night

prime importance. Figures are made recognizable by lines, outlines, and surfaces, but also through relations of light. So, repeatedly in the wide, gray-black nighttime shots of Chicago, we can make out bridges, water, and skyscrapers, or just areas of urban agglomeration, through their mirror images, gradations of light, and reflections. The City Lights in this film are graphic phenomena; in the calm longer shots, they may even become events in themselves. At one point, for example, the camera picks out a distant, flickering string of headlights in the night darkness, when suddenly, out of their midst, a blazing ball of light rises up. Only that movement tells us that the blaze of light is an airborne object and the string of lights is the takeoff runway of an airport. Another moment, the camera waits on a narrow, snow-covered street in front of a row of one-family homes. Finally, a car emerges from a driveway, turns, and drives slowly toward the observer. As the headlights shine directly into the camera, the nighttime street scene is obliterated, but for just an instant, we can see that it's snowing.

The colors in this film are the colors of night, discernible only in conjunction with light. Mostly, they are the colors of signals in the non-places, transmitted via traffic lights, headlights and taillights, neon lettering and advertising signs that stand out against the gray-black darkness. On the "readymade" stages of big-city display windows, still other gradations come into play. It is not by accident that Eisenberg devotes three precisely framed shots to the "Grand Ballroom", a ground-floor reception hall that directs the gaze to either side. White department store dummies and black and white screens are here apparently the décor for a photographic, perhaps festive, stage setting. In the third shot, we see a young woman posing in a red evening dress. The color is caught again briefly in the glass window, with the reflection of a passing car's taillights.

While *Something More Than Night* doesn't show historical, 'anthropological' sites with identifiable names, and while the sound track includes snatches of conversation or loudspeaker announcements but never anything relating to the spaces we see in the visual image, it is definitely not a film without words. As Marc Augé emphasizes, it is precisely the non-places that are filled with banal utopias and clichés; they keep alive the myth of another, better world with their inscriptions and advertising texts. Gigantic billboards, directional signs, and posters determine the contemporary urban landscape. Sometimes even the non-place is defined by the accompanying rules of language, by means of directional signs and instructions for use, whether prescriptive, prohibitive, or informational.[15] The film demonstrates this with multi-layered framings and hieroglyphic images in which inscriptions appear like the parts of a metropolitan rebus, reinforced by the simultaneous presentation of interior and exterior or the equal attention given by the camera to foreground and background.

Twice, the image of night scenes shot near currency exchanges is framed in such a way that each time we see only parts of the words "Currency" and "Exchange". Both times the camera has been set up at an intersection.[16] The first shot is centered on a busy street corner in front of an exchange office; the viewer tries to make the connection between the not entirely legible neon sign and the line of people behind the glass, seemingly unconcerned with the flow of traffic in the foreground. The second fragment, much later in the film, shows another exchange office, whose truncated sign appears in an entirely different context. Here, in the center of the

picture, we see a gigantic lighted billboard advertising DNA tests, visible from far above the rooftops. "Who's the father?" it asks; and here the question is paired with "Currency", a reference to money, making a thought-image reminiscent of Benjamin.

The film's construction sharply contradicts the mythological promise of a genealogy. Its fractures and lines strive for a new set of connections, allowing no fixed positions. According to the terms of Deleuze and Guattari, the film "forms a rhizome". Unlike the family tree with its roots, the rhizome, according to Deleuze and Guattari, is an anti-genealogy.[17] Eisenberg's linking of shots doesn't present us with a focused picture of the city of Chicago, but rather a circulation of nighttime conditions: the courses of movement, transitions from gray shadow to areas of color, architectural lines, or variations of light between the materials of ground, air, and water, followed through in the urban realm as reflections on glass, fog, or steel. The film functions rhizomatically in several directions, not unrelated to *A Thousand Plateaus*. According to Deleuze and Guattari's notion of a cartographic principle, as opposed to a tracing, it is a matter of connecting the external in the heterogeneous, rather than of reproducing a world.[18] In this non-hierarchical system there is no center.

There is no center, but there is such a thing as the film's punctum, namely the close-up of a sleeping child, dropped in like a meteorite between a flickering shot of the lighted city and a dispassionate view into the kitchen of a hot dog stand. While the adults in this film are mostly sleepless people who inhabit the night as nomads or workers waiting for morning to come, one being rests here undisturbed, without changing position. Like all the other persons in *Something More Than Night*, the person in this fragment also remains nameless. The camera shoots from above, the little boy is lying on his back, one arm slightly bent, his hand pointed toward his face. It is the only close-up in the film and, in contrast to all the other fragments, a nearly silent shot. It lasts almost an entire minute and serves as the film's point of rest in every sense, for we hear and see the little boy's regular breathing; he appears to be drifting in another world. This scene functions like a prism for the whole film. One of the intertitles from Eisenberg's *Cooperation of Parts* carried the message: "The eyes are always children."

Rather than attempt a reading of this innermost of all gazes, let us offer one more poem by Celan, one we could call, like that punctum, an ode to a nocturnal face: Vor dein spätes Gesicht,/allein-/gängerisch zwischen/auch mich verwandelnden Nächten,/kam etwas zu stehn,/das schon einmal bei uns war, un-/berührt von Gedanken. (Before your late face/a loner/wandering between nights/that change me too/ something came to stand,/which was with us once already, un-/touched by thoughts.)[19]

With its almost wordless poetics, Daniel Eisenberg's *Something More Than Night* likewise penetrates into an affective realm (of the artist and of the viewer), at once undisturbed and yet profoundly connected to thought.

Translated by Michael Ritterson.

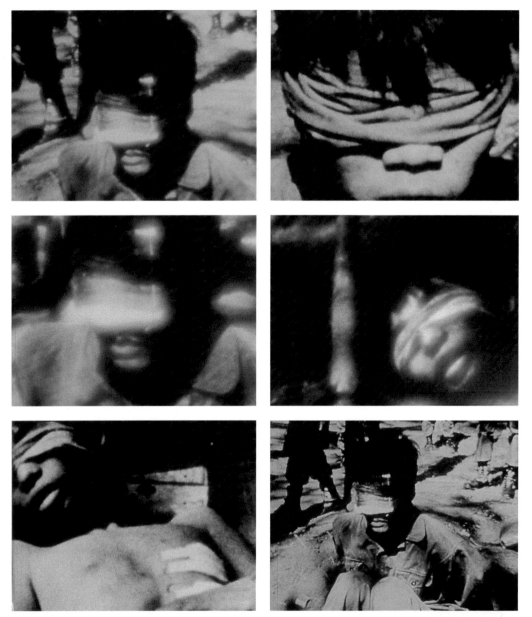

To a Brother in Asia,
Daniel Eisenberg, 1984

POSTWAR

Daniel Eisenberg

I.

[Our] solidarity is the impossible passion one stranger can feel for another.

Edmond Jabès, *The Book of Questions*

These stills, from *To A Brother In Asia*, come from optically printed news footage taken in mid-April, 1975. For almost two weeks, the Vietnamese People's Army and their Viet Cong allies engaged the South Vietnamese Army at Xuan Loc in the last battle of the Vietnam War, where all sides would suffer thousands of casualties. On 29 April, tanks of the People's Army of Vietnam would enter the Presidential Palace in Saigon.

I am looking at these images 35 years after they were taken, and 27 years after working closely with them as an editor of a television documentary about the final days of the Vietnam War. These images of the last dazed teenagers to be taken prisoner in a war that lasted decades, blindfolded and paraded before the international press during the battle have stayed with me. Given the repetition of so much similar imagery that we're subjected to in all the wars we're allowed to see, the blindfolded prisoner, the falling statue, the evacuation of the wounded, and so many others, these should not have such extraordinary resonance—but they do.

Prisoners feeling the dance of sunlight and the shadows of leaves on their blindfolds; the feeding of soup to a gravely wounded soldier, one slow spoon at a time; the bewildered look into the camera of a small boy as he is being lifted by his crying father onto the deck of a freighter in Nha Trang. In the images that flowed from the archive to the editing room, I was particularly taken by such insignificant moments. Deprived of any narrative purpose, they were most often deemed superfluous—outs. I often insisted on including some of them in the cut of the film, precisely because they communicated something outside the boundaries of narrative and time. They maintained an uncanny relationship to history, and that uncanniness came from the combination of two dissonant effects.

First, in these depictions of individuals at the edge of conflict, one immediately recognizes the singularity and ephemerality of these subjects and events, while at the same time being profoundly aware of their eternal repetition, even in our own time. At that moment of our identification with the subject, historical time is ruptured, and we see these people and these events in the present, outside their historical frame. Their moment and ours are one, as the archival image transcends and transgresses the historical. The most famous dramatization of this phenomenon occurs in Roberto Rossellini's *Voyage to Italy*, 1953, when Ingrid Bergman breaks down upon seeing the cast corpses, frozen at the instant of their sudden death, at the ruins of Pompeii. Her utterance, "Life is so short", echoes at once the banality and profound truth of this identification.

Secondly, there is a constant negotiation between the viewer with the subject. At these moments when the divide between past and present is breached, one feels self-consciously voyeuristic for looking, as much as the subjects communicate an equivalent self-consciousness for having been recorded or observed. In the case of these blindfolded prisoners, that self-consciousness remains solely ours.

In retrospect, I can see my attachment to these images at the periphery of history as part of a larger act of recuperation. I projected them onto moments in my own family history for which I had no images, an enterprise I unconsciously repeated in different ways in a number of films over several years. Coming of age at a time when the home movie and the personal archival was at the center of so many critical conversations, I became acutely aware of the lack of images and clear narratives in my own family past. My film work made attempts to address that lack, by emphatically noting that void, or by replacing the void with images that might evoke those that were never made.

Also, as a child, whenever I saw archival images in documentaries on the screen or on television of the Second World War or of the concentration camps, I was invariably drawn to the figures and details at the periphery of the frame or behind the main action. Before video, you had to develop strategies to glean as much as possible from an image, never knowing if you would ever be able to see it again. This was hardly an analytical procedure. It was an attempt to see as much as one possibly could in a fleeting image, in the vain hope of perhaps seeing someone who I might know, or of finding a detail that could perhaps tell me something of my family's life during or before the war. The archive became the site of my psychological desire to see the past, and held the illusory hope of some satisfaction or closure. In that construct, the archive allows for the opportunity to complete the picture, even if the images are those of another narrative and other histories. It is the site where the unconscious finds expression—through literary and photographic means.

The archive makes it plain that narrative and historical meaning are materially and linguistically bound; that these material representations create forms experienced in time. That we have the ability to project secondary meanings and reverberant histories on these images is evidence that the archive is the site of historical construction itself.

Let me return to the image of the blindfolded prisoner for a moment, to indulge a voyeuristic luxury, a profane fantasy.... Could he be thinking of his family, his fate, the warmth of the dappled sunlight on his eyelids? What could possibly be going on in the mind of someone who can't see or know that he is on the precipice of history? That knowledge remains ours alone—knowing what will come in just a few short days after these images were shot.

This moment "just before" is mirrored in the film, *Persistence*, by two moments "just after", the two superimposed moments of the 'year zero' just after the Second World War, and the 'year zero' after the fall of the Berlin Wall. Just as physicists study the traces of subatomic particles accelerated in ever-increasing velocities to get infinitesimally closer to an understanding of the creation of the universe, I am similarly attracted to these images, these traces, as my own universe was created in such a moment of catastrophe.

II.

The recent past always presents itself as if destroyed by catastrophes.

Theodor Adorno, *Minima Moralia*

For over a half-century, the word post-war reverberated with specific meaning, with the absolutes of the Holocaust, Hiroshima, and Nagasaki as part of that meaning. But beyond the specifics of time and place, there's another Postwar... the one that inhabits us. That state of mind was formed in the period just after catastrophe, and its most salient feature was the distinct possibility of yet another, more complete annihilation. Next time all humanity would be its victim. This immanence had a specific valence, attached to vast hierarchical systems of military, economic, and political power. And that real threat of accidental or intentional disaster was either internalized, or expressed through art and politics. With the twin thresholds of the fall of the Berlin Wall and 9/11, we have no doubt passed into yet another paradigm. But it is worth noting some essential aspects of the state of mind that produced the cultural response of that time, which addressed the universalist claims of the modernist fantasy that came before.

Jean-François Lyotard is instructive here, as he convincingly asserts in *The Postmodern Condition* that the unifying "grand narratives" of progress, reward, and redemption cannot possibly hold. If the period preceding ours operated under such narrative assumptions (fascist and Stalinist ideologies being their most extreme and narrow forms), then the twentieth century catastrophes of the Holocaust, the Gulag, and the bomb are the primary evidence of their fallacy.

With our naïve arrival into a world that is already fragmented and in ruin, it takes quite some time to realize that this fragmentation is to us a normative condition. Having never assumed the world to operate under these specious narratives in any case, we also have learned that the catastrophe is neither fully understandable nor describable, and that every effort to describe it, in some way extends our distance from it even further.

Our finely-tuned skepticism to the possibility of comprehension, conditioned by both the incomprehensibility of events and the inadequacies of documentation and testimony, extends to a skepticism of language itself—what it can and cannot convey— since every unknown that precedes us can only be known to us through the imperfect and contingent exchange of words and images.

Since our sense of narrative has been constructed from the fragmented shards of multiple narratives, there is a natural affinity to open forms, difficult structures, multiple interpretations, divergences, and diversity. This esthetic formulation seeks to express an understanding of a cultural condition that is larger than one's own state of mind. It is not purely an expression, but also an analysis, and by extension, a critique.

These tendencies are not bred of theory, but of experience. But all this too, has changed....

III.

'All this talk of getting back to normal', he said of the September terrorist attacks. 'What's normal is now. What was not normal was before. This is the reality of our world. It's the same experience all over, but here in Europe the experience of being vulnerable has existed for hundreds of years. People have somehow become used to living with it.'
Christoph von Dohnanyi (nephew of Dietrich Bonhoeffer, former music director of the Cleveland Orchestra)

The economic precarity that many Europeans accept as the new normal, has since the economic collapse of 2008, become an even more common global condition. That precarity, borne of part-time labor and an increasing economic insecurity, has expanded to include a precarious sense of physical security, political agency, and social stability as well. The insecurity that comes from living under such constraints produces a future that is foreshortened, with the fear that some unknown event, perhaps even the next catastrophe, may be just around the corner.

Every train station, every airport, every bridge, every hotel, auditorium and concert hall, every passage and thoroughfare, every site of entrance and egress, each has the potential for disaster or normalcy, each becomes the site of our new consciousness, reducing every moment and every site to a present that must be contended with, either in acceptance or resistance.

In this environment, and with a new and seemingly endless kind of war being waged simultaneously, one asks: Has the Postwar ended?

War, it seems, happens to others elsewhere. Those who fight it in our name are professionalized from their very first day, and when they are injured or die, it is only their families that pay the price. As George Bush said without irony... our job is to go shopping. Most often, war is neither declared nor defined, it is conceived as outside national borders, and the enemies are non-state actors. In this surreal matrix, war becomes an ever-increasingly abstract, mediated concept.

Unlike the images from Vietnam, which demanded direct response as thousands of the drafted came home wounded or dead, the few images of the current wars that we are able to see now are even further at the edges, and more extreme—whether it is the image coming from a predator drone, or from a cell phone on the streets of Tehran. And we are equally powerless to either protest the employment of these high-tech weapons, managed by out-sourced non-governmental employees in their suburban Virginia bunkers, targeting sites in countries we are not at war with; or to assist the citizens of Tehran who challenge the impossible conditions of dictatorship by daring to face armed agents on their streets. This insulation of events, either intentionally or unintentionally, from the possibility of direct response is a signal characteristic of our time.

What these contemporary images coming to us through both authorized and unauthorized sources demand, as they always have, is a political and emotional analysis that is able to counter the reflexive alienation that now comes packaged with them. The present is now sufficiently encoded that it requires of us the powers of analysis, discipline, and attention formerly reserved for archival images. By actively looking at their edges, these images will eventually tell us what we need to know. The images have it all in them... it is ours to find out.

When producing images of our own, for some future archive, those following us must always be kept in mind, since they will be required to rethink their past (our present) in as nuanced a way as possible, if only to understand their own *presentness* in its fullness. The images we produce now, will have more meaning than we are able to imagine.

Perhaps the acceptance of the "long war" as a condition of daily life means we now need to rethink "Postwar" as a utopian concept... again, for a time just after.

... Will we be able to recognize it when it comes?

Comment vivre sans inconnu devant soi? (How can we live without the unknown before us?)

Rene Char, *Argument*

Saigon, Vietnam,
May, 1975

END NOTES

PERSISTENT DISPLACEMENTS:
THE CITY FILMS OF DAN EISENBERG

1 Plato, *The Collected Dialogues of Plato: Including the Letters*, Edith Hamilton, ed., Princeton: Princeton University Press, 1971, p. 520.
2 Benjamin, Walter, *Selected Wrtings Vol 4 1938–1940*, Howard Eiland and Michael W. Jennings, eds., Cambridge MA: Harvard University Press, 2003, p. 392.
3 Sitney, P. Adams, "*Interview with Stan Brakhage*", *Film Culture Reader*, P. A. Sitney, ed., New York: Cooper Square Press, 2000, p. 202.
4 Kracauer, Siegfried, *The Mass Ornament: Weimar Essays*, Thomas Y. Levin, trans. and ed., Cambridge MA: Harvard University Press, 1995, p. 139.

KIDS ON A BIKE

1 The first three shots last about 40 frames while the fourth lasts more than 50.
2 Daniel Eisenberg has underlined the strong personal implications of this film in an interview with the filmmaker Peter Delpeut, in his documentary essay "The Time Machine", 1996. He remembers how moved he was when he learned, while watching Marcel Ophüls' *The Sorrow and the Pity*, 1969, that Hitler, while visiting the church of the Madeleine in Paris, had stopped at the very spot where he had sat down as an adolescent during a trip to Paris. "Without him", he adds, "I wouldn't exist since my parents met after the war in a camp of Displaced Persons at Dachau."

SOUND SCORES: MUSICAL ARMATURE
IN *DISPLACED PERSON*

1 Eisenberg, Daniel, "Daniel Eisenberg im Gespräch Mit Alf Bold", *Kinemathek*, 29, January 1992, p. 7.
2 See Benjamin, Walter, "Theoretics of Knowledge: Theory of Progress", *The Philosophical Review*, 15, 1–2, 1983–1984, p. 24.
3 Adorno, Theodor W., "The Essay as Form", 1954–1958 in *Notes to Literature*, vol. 1, New York: Columbia University Press, 1993.
4 For background on the essay film see my "Translating the Essay into Film and Installation", *Journal of Visual Culture*, 6:1, April 2007, pp. 45–58.
5 Doane, Mary Ann, *The Emergence of Cinematic Time:*

Modernity, Contingency, the Archive, Cambridge MA: Harvard University Press, 2002, p. 25.
6 Rancière, Jacques, *The Future of an Image*, London: Verso, 2007, p. 127.
7 See Alan Sekula on the archive: Sekula, Alan, "Reading an Archive: Photography Between Labour and Capital", *The Photography Reader*, Liz Wells, ed., New York: Routledge, 2002, pp. 443–452.
8 For an essay on Ophüls' vexed relationship with Germany see my "Marcel Ophüls', November Days: German Reunification as Musical Comedy", *Film Quarterly*, 51, Winter 1998, pp. 32–43.
9 Frampton's film is composed of a series of still photographs each of which are held on the screen while a voice-over describes in detail not what is currently visible on the screen but an image that will come. A temporal disjunct is therefore created between what is seen and what is described.
10 The lecture is published in *Myth and Meaning: Cracking the Code of Culture*, Toronto: University of Toronto Press, 1978.
11 See Benjamin, Walter, "The Task of the Translator", 1923, *Illuminations*, New York: Schocken Books, 1969.
12 For a detailed analysis the translatability of the written form of the essay into an audio-visual medium see my "Translating the Essay into Film and Installation". Cited above.
13 Rancière, Jacques. *The Future of an Image*, London: Verso, 2007, p. 111.
14 Rodowick, D.N., *The Virtual Life of Film*, Cambridge MA: Harvard University Press, 2007, p. 74.
15 Calvalcanti, Alberto, "Sound in Films", *Film Sound: Theory and Practice*, Elisabeth Weis and John Belton eds., Columbia University Press, 1985, p. 109.
16 Gorbman, Claudia. *Unheard Melodies: Narrative Film Music*, Bloomington: Indiana University Press, 1987, p. 7.
17 Chion, Michel, "Mute Music: Polanski's the Pianist and Campion's the Piano", *Beyond the Soundtrack: Representing Music in Cinema*, Goldmark, Daniel, Lawrence Kramer and Richard Leppert eds., Berkeley: University of California Press, 2007, p. 91.
18 Leppert in response to Adorno on Wagner's relevancy. In Adorno, Theodor, *Essays on Music*. Richard Leppert ed., with an introduction and commentary. Berkeley: University of California Press, 2002, p. 535.
19 See for example the fate of the Polish bundist leaders Viktor Alter and Henryk Ehrlich who after years of imprisonment were eventually executed by Stalin.
20 Kramer, Lawrence, *Musical Meaning: Toward a Critical History*, Berkeley: University of California Press, 2002, p. 4.

21 Bitmosky, Hartmut, "Slash/Dash", *In Uncharted Territory:
Essays on Early Nonfiction Film*, Daan Hertogs and Nico de
Klerk ed., Amsterdam: Nederlands Film Museum, 1997,
pp. 61–74, 67.

FOLIO SECTION
Displaced Person
pp. 66–71.

FRAGMENTS OF AN INHERITANCE: CONTINGENCES OF HISTORY IN *COOPERATION OF PARTS*

1 Eisenberg, Daniel, "Filmscript of *Cooperation of Parts*
& Commentaries" *Kinemathek*, 77, January 1992, Berlin:
Freunde der Deutschen Kinemathek, p. 49.
2 Hirsch, Marianne, *Family Frames: Photography, Narrative,
and Postmemory*, Cambridge MA: Harvard University Press,
1997, p. 22.
3 McElhatten, Mark, "Dan Eisenberg's *Cooperation of Parts*",
Kinemathek, 77, January 1992, Berlin: Freunde der Deutschen
Kinemathek, p. 31.
4 Eisenberg, "Filmscript of *Cooperation of Parts* &
Commentaries", p. 49.
5 Eisenberg, "Filmscript of *Cooperation of Parts* &
Commentaries", p. 61.
6 For an important theoretical discussion of the lyrical
camera style see P. Adams Sitney, *Modernist Montage:
The Obscurity of Vision in Cinema and Literature*, New York:
Columbia University Press, 1992. See especially pp. 196–210.
7 Eisenberg, "Filmscript of *Cooperation of Parts* &
Commentaries", pp. 45 and 49.
8 Eisenberg, "Filmscript of *Cooperation of Parts* &
Commentaries", p. 49.
9 To sideshadow in the creation of historical narrative is to
illuminate other aspects that exist simultaneously as part
of the main trajectory of an event showing the density in the
dynamics of that history. As the literary critic Michael André
Bernstein suggests, to sideshadow is to also look at what
did not happen in an historical event, as well as what did,
what might have happened but didn't, and importantly, what
else happened and continues to. Sideshadowing opens the
possibility for narrative forms which can render events in all
their complexity rather than binaristic narratives of cause
and effect which are so often reductive and simplistic. In
contrast, sideshadowing builds counter-narratives into
the central narrative of a history to offer events and ideas which
raise the notion of multiple contingencies and possible
alternatives for understanding events in a history. When
sideshadowed possibilities become part of the narrative, it
gives the sense that history has no inevitable outcome or
closure because so many things are happening simultaneously.
For the complete discussion of his concept of shadowing
and its literary implications, see Michael André Bernstein's
Forgone Conclusions: Against Apocalyptic History, Berkeley:
University of California Press, 1994.
10 This issue of the use of testimony and personal experience
in avant-garde film is taken up in more depth in my book
*Shadows, Specters, Shards: Making History in Avant-
Garde Film*, Minneapolis: University of Minnesota Press
2005, see especially chapter 4 "Specters: The Limits of
Representing History".
11 Minh-Ha, Trinh T., "Documentary Is/Not a Name", *October*,
52, Spring, 1990, p. 77.

Elements of this essay have appeared in substantially
different form in my book *Shadows, Specters, Shards:
Making History in Avant-Garde Film*, Minneapolis:
University of Minnesota Press, 2005.

FOLIO SECTION
Cooperation of Parts
pp. 92–97.

LOOKING ACROSS THE THRESHOLD: *PERSISTENCE* AS EXPERIMENT IN TIME, SPACE, AND GENRE

1 An important exception to this generalization is Robert
A. Rosenstone who has written and edited a number of
important books that argue not only for using film to do
history but also for the unique contribution such histories
make. See his introduction to *Revisioning History: Film
and the Construction of a New Past*, Princeton: Princeton
University Press, 1995), pp. 3–14 and his *Visions of the Past*,
Cambridge MA: Harvard Univ. Press, 1995) and *History on
Film/Film on History*, London: Pearson/Longman, 2006,
Marc Ferro, *Cinéma et Histoire*, Paris: Editions Denoel,
1977. Pierre Sorlin, *The Film in History: Restaging the Past*,
Totowa, N J Barnes and Noble, 1980) and his piece in
Revisioning History, "The Night of the Shooting Stars: Fascism,
Resistance, and the Liberation of Italy", pp. 77–88.
2 This debate is well-summarized in Novick, Peter, *That Noble
Dream: The 'Objectivity Question' and the American Historical*

Profession, Cambridge: Cambridge University Press, 1988.
Two influential critics of the possibility of truth-telling were
Hayden G. White. See among other texts, *Metahistory: The
Historical Imagination in Nineteenth-century Europe*, Baltimore:
Johns Hopkins, 1973, and Dominic LaCapra, see, *History and
Criticism*, Ithaca: Cornell University Press, 1985.
3 A survey of the articles appearing in both publications of
the American Historical Association, *Perspectives* and *The
American Historical Review* will confirm this point. On the
one hand, the main organization of professional historians
in the United States has acknowledged the importance
of film by establishing conference sessions on film and
history, a prize for the best documentary film, and regular
rubrics on the topic in both publications but vast majority
of the work published there discusses either conventionally
documentary films or televisions series or mass-market
films and assess the accuracy or effectiveness of their
presentation of history.
4 Lodkowsi, Mariusz, "Battle over a suitcase from Auschwitz",
Sunday Times, 13 August, 2006.
5 Riding, Alan, "The Fight over a Suitcase and the Memories
it Carries", *New York Times*, 16 September, 2006; Ceaux,
Pascal, *Le Monde*, 2 September, 2006. On this institution see:
"Archiving a Life: Post-*Shoah* Paradoxes of Memory Legacies",
in *Unsettling Histories*, Alf Lüdtke and Sebastien Jobs eds.,
Frankfurt: Campus Verlag, forthcoming.
6 Auslander, "Archiving a Life".
7 Auslander, Leora, *Taste and Power: Furnishing Modern
France*, Berkeley: University of California Press, 1996;
Introduction, "Accommodation, Resistance, and Eigensinn:
Evolués and Sapeurs between Africa and Europe", in Belinda
Davis and Michael Wildt eds., *Alltag, Erfahurng, Eigensinn:
Historisch-Anthropologische Erkundungen*, Frankfurt/New
York: Campus Verlag, 2008, pp. 205–217.
8 This discussion echoes, in many ways, that of Jeffrey
Skoller in *Shadows, Specters, Shards: Making History in
Avant-Garde Film*, Minneapolois: University of Minnesota
Press, 2005.
9 See particularly Ladd, Brian,*The Ghosts of Berlin: Confronting
German History in the Urban Landscape*, Chicago: University
of Chicago Press, 1997.
10 As far as I know the first use of the concept in this way
is Huyssen, Andreas, "Present Pasts: Media, Politics, and
Amnesia", *Public Culture*, 12, no. 1, 2000: pp. 21–38 and his
Present Pasts : Urban Palimpsests and the Politics of History,
Stanford: Stanford University Press, 2003.

THE PERSISTENCE OF THE ARCHIVE:
THE DOCUMENTARY FICTIONS OF DANIEL EISENBERG

1 Foucault, Michel, "The History of Sexuality", interviewer
Lucette Finas, in *Power/Knowledge: Selected Interviews and
Other Writings: 1972–1977*, Colin Gordon ed., Colin Gordon, Leo
Marshall, John Mepham and Kate Soper, trans., New York:
Pantheon, 1980, p. 192.
2 Deleuze, Gilles, *Foucault*, Seán Hand trans., Minneapolis:
Minnesota University Press, 1988, p. 120.
3 Skoller, Jeffrey, *Shadows, Specters and Shards: Making
History in Avant-Garde Film*, Minneapolis: Minnesota University
Press, 2005, p. 84.
4 On the relationship of these films to his biography, see
Bold, Alf, "Displaced Persons: Dan Eisenberg Interviewed",
Millennium Film Journal, 27, Winter 1993–1994, pp. 48–63.
5 On Eisenberg's use of this technique in *Persistence*, see
Skoller, p. 88.

This essay is a substantially rewritten excerpt from an
essay originally commissioned by the Video Data Bank for
the DVD *Film and Video Works by Dan Eisenberg*.

FOLIO SECTION
Persistence
pp. 138–149.

NON-PLACES, NOMADS, AND NAMELESS ONES:
NOTES ON *SOMETHING MORE THAN NIGHT*

1 Celan, Paul, "Night", *Speech-Gille and Selected Poems*,
Joachim Neugroschel trans., New York: Dutton, 1970.
2 Deleuze, Gilles and Félix Guattari, *A Thousand Plateaus.
Capitalism & Schizophrenia*, Minneapolis: University of
Minnesota Press, 1987, pp. 3–25, pp. 12–15.
3 Augé, Marc, *Non-Places: Introduction to an Anthropology of
Supermodernity*, London: Verso, 1995, p. 78.
4 de Certeau, Michel, *The Practice of Everyday Life*, Berkeley:
University of California Press, 1984, p. 117, quoted from Augé,
Non-Places, p. 80.
5 Augé, *Non-Places*, p. 83ff.
6 Deleuze describes the transformation of power, as
Foucault understands it for the disciplinary society, as
the breakup of the traditional coupling mass-individual.
"Individuals become 'dividuals', and masses become
samples, data, markets, or 'banks'." Deleuze, Gilles

"Postscript on Control Societies", *Negotiations*, New York: Columbia University Press, 1995, pp. 177–182, p. 180.

7 Augé, *Non-Places*, p. 94.

8 See shots 25, 26 and 27.

9 Lefebvre, Jean-Pierre, "Préface", in Paul Celan, *Choix de Poèmes*, trans. into French and presented by Jean-Pierre Lefebvre, bilingual edition, Paris: Gallimard, 1998, p. 11.

10 On the family background and historical context of the "Displaced Persons", Daniel Eisenberg et al. in conversation with Alf Bold, *Hefte der Deutschen Kinemathek*, 77, Daniel Eisenberg, 29, 1992, pp. 4–17, pp. 11–12.

11 See for example shots 37 and 63.

12 Celan, Paul, "Flooding, big", *Glottal Stop: 101 Poems*, Nikolai Popov and Heather McHugh trans., Middletown: Wesleyan University Press, 2004.

13 Michel Foucault defines this theory of spaces or heterotopology in "Of Other Spaces", Jay Miskowiec trans., *Diacritics*, 16:1, pp. 22–27.

14 See shot 32.

15 Augé, *Non-Places*, p. 104.

16 See shots 40 and 62.

17 Deleuze and Guattari, *A Thousand Plateaus*, p. 10. Shortly therafter, on p. 11, the two delineate their program: "Write, form a rhizome, increase your territory by deterritorialization, extend the line of flight to the point where it becomes an abstract machine covering the entire plane of consistency."

18 Deleuze and Guattari, *A Thousand Plateaus*, p. 35.

19 Celan, Paul "Before Your Late Face", *Breathturn*, Pierre Joris trans., Los Angeles: Sun and Moon Press, 1995.

FOLIO SECTION
Something More Than Night
pp. 166–171.

INDEX

CONTRIBUTING WRITERS

NORA M. ALTER

Nora M. Alter is Professor and Chair of the Department of Film andMedia Arts at Temple University. She is author of *Vietnam Protest Theatre: The Television War on Stage*, 1996, *Projecting History: Non-Fiction German Film*, 2002, *Chris Marker*, 2006, and is co-editor with Lutz Koepnick of *Sound Matters: Essays on the Acoustics of Modern German Culture*, 2004. She has contributed essays to collections on film, cultural studies, and visual studies and published articles in journals including *Camera Obscura*, *Cultural Critique*, *New German Critique*, *The Germanic Revue*, *Film Quarterly* and serves on the editorial board of "The Germanic Quarterly" Foundation. In 2005 she was awarded the DAAD Prize for Distinguished Scholarship in German and European Studies. She is currently completely a new book on the international essay film.

LEORA AUSLANDER

Leora Auslander is Professor of European Social History at the University of Chicago. She specializes in the history of France and Germany, focusing on nineteenth and twentieth century social history; material culture and consumption and Jewish History. She is the author of *Cultural Revolutions: Everyday Life and Politics in Britain, North America, and France*, 2009, and *Taste and Power: Furnishing Modern France* (Studies on the History of Society and Culture), 1998.

Auslander was a Berthold Leibinger Fellow at the American Academy in Berlin, Germany, for Fall 2008. From 1996 to 1999, she served as Director of the Center for Gender Studies at the University of Chicago. Auslander's most recent area of research is at the intersection of Jewish history and material culture on which she has published widely. Her forthcoming book is *Strangers at Home: Jewish Parisians and Berliners in the Twentieth Century*.

RAYMOND BELLOUR

Raymond Bellour is Director of Research at the Centre National de la Recherche Scientifique and Professor at the Centre Universitaire Américain de Cinéma in Paris. He is the author and editor of a dozen books on literature, film, cultural criticism, and critical theory. He has long been recognized as one of the leading proponents of the "textual analysis" of film, and several of his essays on Hitchcock are internationally regarded as groundbreaking meditations on the relation between psychoanalysis, narrative, and spectacle. Since the early 80s his work has concentrated on mixed media and the relation between words and images. *Passages de l'image*, 1989, a book, *L'Entre-Images*, 1990, and a MOMA catalog, *Jean-Luc Godard: Sonimage*,1992, Bellour is also co-editor of the cinema journal *Trafic* which he started in 1991, with Serge Daney.

CHRISTA BLÜMLINGER

Christa Blümlinger is Maître de Conférences at the Université Sorbonne Nouvelle, Paris III (Film and Media Studies) She is also a writer, art critic and curator and has written for many magazines including *Trafic*, *Cinémathèque*, *Iris*, *Balthazar*, *Montage AV* and *Meteor* (on cinema), *Springerin*, *Eikon*, *Camera Austria*, *Texte zur Kunst* and *Parachute* (on contemporary art). She has curated various film and video programs at festivals such as Duisburger Filmwoche, Diagonale and Arsenal. Her most recent books include the critical edition of writings by Serge Daney *Von der Welt ins Bild. Augenzeugenberichte eines Cinephilen*, 2000, *Das Gesicht im Zeitalter des bewegten Bildes*, 2002 (with Karl Sierek), the critical edition of writings by Harun Farocki *Reconnaître et poursuivre*, 2002, and her new book on the (re)use of "found footage" in cinema and new media was published in 2007.

SCOTT DURHAM

Scott Durham is Associate Professor of French and Chair of the Department of French and Italian at Northwestern University, where he also teaches Comparative Literary Studies. He is the author of *Phantom Communities: The Simulacrum and the Limits of Postmodernism*, and the editor of a *Yale French Studies*issue on Jean Genet. He is currently writing two books, with the working titles *Eurydice's Gaze: Historicity, Memory and Untimeliness in Postmodern Film and The Archive* and the *Monad: Deleuze and the Resistance to Postmodernism*.

TOM GUNNING

Tom Gunning is the Edwin A. Bergman and Betty L. Bergman Distinguished Service Professor of Art History and Chair of the Department of Cinema & Media Studies. He is the author of *The Films of Fritz Lang: Allegories of Vision and Modernity*, 2000, and *D.W. Griffith and the Origins of American Narrative Film: The Early Years at Biograph*, 1991. His published work of over hundred publications has concentrated on early cinema, as well as on the culture of modernity from which cinema arose. He has also written extensively on the Avant-Garde film, both in its European pre-First World War manifestations and the American Avant-Garde film up to the present day.

JEFFREY SKOLLER

Jeffrey Skoller, Associate Professor of Film Studies at the University of California, Berkeley, is a filmmaker and writer. Skoller has made over a dozen films that have been exhibited in museums, universities and festivals internationally. Screenings and exhibitions include: The Pacific Film Archive, Berkeley; Portland Art Museum, OR., The Gene Siskel Film Center, Art Institute of Chicago, The S. F. Cinematheque; Museum of the Moving Image, N.Y., J. P. Getty Museum, Los Angeles, CA., Whitney Museum; N.Y.; P.S. 1, N.Y., Flaherty Film Seminar, N.Y.; Arsenal Kino, Berlin; Mannheim Film Festival, Germany; The Latin American Film Festival, Havana; National Film Theatre, London. His essays and articles on experimental film and video have appeared in *Film Quarterly*; *Discourse*; *Afterimage*; *Cinematograph*; *New Art Examiner* among others. He is the author of the book, *Shadows*, *Specters*, *Shards: Making History in Avant-Garde Film*, 2005.

DANIEL EISENBERG

Daniel Eisenberg has been making films and videos for the past 30 years. His films have been screened throughout Europe and North America with solo exhibitions at the Museum of Modern Art, N.Y.C., the Centre Georges Pompidou, Paris, the Pacific Film Archive, Berkeley, the American Museum of the Moving Image in New York, the Musée du Cinema, Brussels; De Unie, Rotterdam; and Kino Arsenal, Berlin. His films have been shown in the Berlin Film Festival; the Sydney Film Festival; the London Film Festival; the Jerusalem Film Festival; Vue Sur Les Docs, Marseilles, and the Whitney Biennial, New York. His work has also been featured in many conferences and symposia, including the first International Walter Benjamin Conference, Portbou-Barcelona, Spain.

Eisenberg's films have won numerous awards, fellowships, and honors. Among these are a John Simon Guggenheim Fellowship; the D.A.A.D. Berliner Künstlerprogramm Fellowship; National Endowment for the Arts Fellowship. Awards include arc+film Festival, Graz; Ann Arbor Film Festival, Black Maria Film and Video Festival, New England Film Festival. His films are in the collections of the Centre Georges Pompidou, Paris, the Freunde der Deutschen Kinemathek, Berlin, the Nederlands Filmmuseum, the Haus des Dokumentarfilm, Stuttgart, the Australian Film and Television School, Sydney.

Eisenberg lives and works in Chicago and is Professor of Film/Video/New Media, and Visual and Critical Studies, at the School of the Art Institute of Chicago.

FILMOGRAPHY

The Incompletist digital video, 2011
The Unstable Object digital video, 2011
Frame-up 7 minutes, digital video, 2007
Far From Here mixed media installation, 2007
Something More Than Night 77 minutes, 16mm, 2003
Persistence 84 minutes, 16mm, 2007
Cooperation of Parts 41 minutes, 16mm, 1987
Film Studies 20 minutes, 16mm, 1979–1990
To a Brother in Asia mixed media, 1983
Native Shore 10 minutes, 16mm, 1983
Displaced Person 12 minutes,16mm, 1981
Design and Debris 11 minutes, 16mm, 1979
Matrice 8 minutes, 8mm/16mm, 1975

16mm films are available through Canyon Cinema, San Francisco, Light Cone, Paris, Freunde Der Deutschen Kinemathek, Berlin, and Daniel Eisenberg Films.

Digital Video and DVD available through the Video Data Bank, Chicago, and Daniel Eisenberg Films

ACKNOWLEDGEMENTS

I am grateful for the opportunity to edit this book, which has given me the privilege of working on Eisenberg's extraordinary films in a way that has deepened my understanding of cinema, art and history. Similarly, I want to thank the brilliant writers included here, who generously shared their ideas and so creatively illuminated these complex films. Working with such accomplished writers on their essays has been a rare privilege. Thanks also go to Will Bishop, Michael Ritterson, Daniel Hendrickson and Brittany Murray, who worked so hard on the difficult translations of the poetic texts by Bellour and Blümlinger. Thank you to Leslie Salzinger for all manner of help—editorial and otherwise. My deepest appreciation to Alex Wright, the graphic designer at Black Dog Publishing, in London who collaborated with us with great patience and creativity in figuring out how the book should be structured. Sincere thanks go to Duncan McCorquodale, Black Dog's publisher, for giving Dan and me the opportunity to make a book of this kind. His vision for a film book that would emphasize the visual aspects of the films with such elaborate interplay between the images and challenging texts is almost unheard of in this day and age of dwindling resources for creative book publishing. Other generous support came from The School of the Art Institute of Chicago and the University of California, Berkeley. Finally my deepest thanks go to Daniel Eisenberg, who trusted me to edit a book on his films. Our collaboration has been a joyful experience of creative exploration. I have learned so much from our endless conversations and debates as we put this book together. My hope is that the book will excite you to explore these brilliant films as deeply as I have.

Jeffrey Skoller, Berkeley, California, 2010

To have some of the finest contemporary writers on cinema reflect on one's work is indeed a rare honor and privilege. I am deeply indebted to their intellectual generosity, which has opened up so many new ways to consider my films. Their work has allowed Jeffrey Skoller and I to rethink the films through and within their texts, and to redefine the terrain of 'the book' at a moment in time when its own definitions—as an object, as a resource, and as a form— are so much in flux. In doing so, we seem to have found some new ways to redefine the terrain of the moving image as well....

None of this would have been possible without the steadfast commitment, support, and guidance of Duncan McCorquodale, who immediately saw the possibilities in the project, and encouraged us from the very start to think at the edge of our own creative power. With humor and patience, Alex Wright, our partner in design, grasped many of the subtexts and themes we were working with, and brought them to eloquent form. I must also thank Stefanie Schulte-Strathaus at Arsenal Experimental in Berlin, and Jana Wright, Dean of Academic Administration, Columbia University, for their early support, and Rüdiger van den Boom and the Goethe-Institute, Chicago, Alan Labb, Associate Dean of Technology at the School of the Art Institute of Chicago, Paige Sarlin, Damla Tokcan-Faro, and Sheryl Ridenour for their efforts here in Chicago.

Jeffrey Skoller, has once again demonstrated why he has been my most valued interlocutor over the years. His deep understanding of the moving image and its history, and his unwavering belief in the future of independent media, has guided this project from the outset. With discipline and rigor, he has kept us true to the book's objectives. The dialectical conversation, the sense of play as well as argument, took us to surprising places along the way, and demonstrated that collaborative authorship is both empowering and liberating. I owe him as much for the time we spent as for the book itself.

Finally, without the support of Ellen Rothenberg not only the book, but many of the films would just not be... she is there, always. It is to her, and to Jesse and Rose that the book is dedicated.

Daniel Eisenberg, Chicago, 2010

COLOPHON

Designed by Alex Wright at Black Dog Publishing.

Black Dog Publishing Limited
10a Acton Street
London WC1X 9NG
United Kingdom

Tel: +44 (0)20 7713 5097
Fax: +44 (0)20 7713 8682
info@blackdogonline.com
www.blackdogonline.com

British Library Cataloguing-in-Publication Data.
A CIP record for this book is available from the
British Library.

ISBN 978 1 906155 95 7

Black Dog Publishing Limited, London, UK,
is an environmentally responsible company.
Postwar is printed on an FSC certified paper.
Printed by Melita Press in Malta.

architecture art design
fashion history photography
theory and things

www.blackdogonline.com